dot.com**dating**

Tyndale House Publishers, Inc. • Carol Stream, Illinois

drs. les & leslie parrott
dot.com**dating**

finding your
right someone
online

*avoiding the liars,
losers, and freaks*

Visit Tyndale's exciting Web site at www.tyndale.com.

Visit Les and Leslie's Web site at www.realrelationships.com.

TYNDALE and Tyndale's quill logo are registered trademarks of Tyndale House Publishers, Inc.

dot.com dating: finding your right someone online—avoiding the liars, losers, and freaks

Designed by Jacqueline L. Nuñez

Edited by Susan Taylor

Scripture quotations are taken from the *Holy Bible*, New Living Translation, copyright © 1996, 2004, 2007 by Tyndale House Foundation. Used by permission of Tyndale House Publishers, Inc., Carol Stream, Illinois 60188. All rights reserved.

Library of Congress Cataloging-in-Publication Data

Parrott, Les.
   dot.com dating : finding your right someone online—avoiding the liars, losers, and freaks / Les Parrott and Leslie Parrott.
       p. cm.
   Includes bibliographical references.
   ISBN 978-1-4143-4865-0 (sc)
   1. Online dating. 2. Mate selection. I. Parrott, Leslie L., date. II. Title.
   HQ801.82.P37 2010
   306.730285—dc22   2010040224

Printed in the United States of America

16 15 14 13 12 11 10
 7   6   5   4   3   2   1

We dedicate this little book to single people

everywhere

who are passionate in their faith and

faithful in their passions.

contents

megapixels and modems— the new normal for dating?

I met my husband online. We lived three streets away from each other but never would have met otherwise.
—VICKIE WAGONER

A MAN SENDS a knowing glance to a woman from across the room. Her head tilts slightly as she sees him. She lifts her shoulders and touches her hair. Their eyes lock for a brief moment. She smiles, then slowly drops her eyelids, tilting her head down and to the side. Volumes of body language are written between them in mere seconds. The exciting spark of mutual interest leads the man to walk toward her and strike up a conversation and possibly ask for a date.

It could happen anywhere: school, church, a party, a restaurant, even standing in line at the grocery store. But these days, for many, those romantic sparks are just as likely to be found *on*line as they are to be found *in* line.

There's no denying it. People are finding their soul mates on the Web as often as they are anywhere else. *More than a third of America's ninety-seven million singles are dating online.* With the click of a mouse, single people are meeting other singles. In fact, more than half of the people who have signed up for an online dating service have been on a date with someone they met online. According to Mark Penn, author of *Microtrends*, one in five Americans in their twenties, and one in ten Americans in their thirties or older are actively looking to find their soul mates online.[1] And the numbers grow larger every day.

Is it working? The answer is an unequivocal *yes*. Singles of all stages and ages are not only finding someone to date; they're also finding matrimony. Every week we hear from happy couples who met in cyberspace and are enjoying marriage together. More than twice as many couples who married last year met through online dating services compared to social events.[2] According to a recent study conducted by a consumer group, one in five people who've used dating sites have gone on to marry someone they met online. That's more than the number of couples in America who say they met in church.[3]

Why We Wrote This Little Book

As a psychologist (Les) and a marriage and family therapist (Leslie), we think a lot about relationships.

We've written more than a dozen books on the topic. We teach university courses on relationships and marriage. On most weekends you'll find us speaking at a relationship seminar, usually in a church, somewhere in North America. We have a Web site (RealRelationships.com) where we provide complimentary video answers to relationship questions people ask when they write to us. We do television, radio, and magazine interviews on relationship issues almost weekly.

Because of all that, we hear from thousands of singles across the country every year. And the question they ask us more than any other is this: Do you think I should try online dating?

The question typically comes from the earnest hearts of people who are genuinely wondering when or if they will find the love of their lives. The heartfelt sincerity behind this often-asked question—which comes from the young and never married as well as from the more mature widowed and divorced—set us on a quest some years ago to research the practice of online dating from every angle. In the end, it resulted in more than just this little book. We'll be up front: It resulted in a compelling call to cofound an online dating site that does something for Christian singles that no other site has done before. We'll fill you in on that, just briefly, at the end of this book.

Our Promise to You

For now, we simply want to give you the information from our research that we believe you'll find helpful when it comes to being smart about this increasingly popular tool of electronic dating. Whether you end up going online to find your special someone or you decide to rely on "old-fashioned" means for finding your romantic sparks, we want to help you improve your "Love IQ" by helping you get savvy about your options. This holds true even if you've already tried online dating and ended up being skeptical.

We've made this book brief and to the point. Each chapter is only a few short pages because we don't want to load you down with unnecessary details. We promise to cut to the heart of the matter by focusing on the following three major issues:

- First, we'll debunk the myths too many people still hold about online dating, typically because they are misinformed or are relying on old information.
- Second, we'll help you determine whether online dating is for you, and we'll show you six ways to know for sure.
- And finally, we'll give you a list of questions you absolutely must ask before you sign up

for any online dating site. We think they could make or break your online dating experience.

Before we leave this introduction, we want you to know something. We've written every word of this book with you in mind. We don't know you, of course, but we *do* know that you are sincere about finding that special someone. You wouldn't read this book if you weren't. We also assume that you could be anywhere from your twenties to late in your more-seasoned years. You may have never been married, or you may be divorced or widowed. We also assume you are a person of high moral standards and you hold a personal Christian faith. You're not looking for the proverbial "hookup"; you're not cruising the club scene. You're holding out for the very best that God has for you. And it's our heartfelt prayer that you will find it—soon. This book is dedicated to helping you do just that.

With every good wish and prayer,

—Les and Leslie Parrott
Seattle, Washington

Part 1

The Six Big Myths of Online Dating

Online
dating has
revolutionized
the way people
find and pursue
potential mates.
—ELLEN MCCARTHY

1

Myth: Online Dating Carries an Embarrassing Stigma

People hear success stories, try it for themselves, shed the stigma, and later proudly announce: "We met on an online dating service."

—JOE TRACY[1]

IT STARTED WITH the very first couple to ever meet online. The year was 1982 when Chris Dunn met Pam Jensen on a CompuServe CB Simulator program. Computer users nationwide were able to be connected in an early version of a chat room. After a few months of virtual chatting, Chris flew from New York to Chicago to meet Pam face-to-face. People said it wouldn't last, and even Chris's father thought it was a joke. But a year later, Chris and Pam exchanged wedding vows.

Their courtship and wedding were featured on numerous television programs and in newspaper articles, including a *New York Times* story titled "Of Bytes and Bulletin Boards."[2] That was more than twenty-five years ago, and Chris and Pam are still in love and happily married.

These days, of course, a couple falling in love online is hardly newsworthy. But Pam and Chris were charting new territory. "At the time," Pam recalls, "computers weren't as pervasive in our homes and our daily life. To a lot of people, especially my parents' generation and their friends, it seemed very alien, a very suspicious concept to even be communicating like that."

Today the couple lives on the north side of Chicago. "If it weren't for the way we met, I think we could be any other married couple," says Chris. "I've always adored her. She adores me. It's very easy to love my wife."[3]

That part may be easy, but from the start, Chris and Pam had to put up with a great deal of suspicion from others. And so have a lot of other couples who have sometimes felt compelled to hide the fact that they met online.

It's Called "Stigma"

"How did you two meet?" The question was posed to a group of newlywed wives at a Sunday school function.

Going around the circle, each took a moment to tell her romantic story. Then it was time for Tracy to speak up: "We met over the Internet."

There was a moment of silence.

Then the teacher commented, "Really! Why would an attractive, outgoing girl like you need to resort to such drastic measures?"

That's "stigma"—a socially discrediting means of classifying others as going against the norm. It's an undesirable stereotype. It conjures up disapproval, disgrace, and shame, and it's based on uninformed impressions.

This Sunday school teacher is a perfect example of someone who perpetuates an uneducated social stigma of online dating. But truth be told, the above exchange took place more than a decade ago. Today, these misinformed impressions about online dating are few and far between.

So if you're embarrassed by an out-of-date stigma of online dating, you've somehow gotten stuck in a fleeting notion that died out years ago. Yes, it used to be that finding love online was looked at with suspicion. But so was nearly everything else about the Internet. After all, this newfangled mechanism is not that old. It was only August 6, 1991, when the first Web site was built to explain what the World Wide Web was and how you could own a browser and set up a Web server. *What?* Most people scoffed at the visionary idea of using our computers to buy shoes, download music, or book a hotel room. So why in the world would anyone look to the Internet to find love?

Of course, that was then. This is now. And today, the stigma of online dating has all but vanished. Everyone knows someone who has found the love of his or her life online. Even well-known celebrities talk about using matching sites to find love. We do enough marriage seminars in churches around the country to know that in every congregation there are couples who proudly identify themselves as having been matched online. Sure, some uninformed holdouts still insist on perpetuating the stigma, but their numbers are dwindling quickly.

Your Grandmother's Internet?

If you're looking for evidence that online dating has all but shaken off any remnants of embarrassing stigma, just look at the generation before yours. You may think that some older people rarely even turn on a computer, but you'd be wrong. We all know how popular online dating is for younger generations, but—are you ready for this?—the fastest-growing group to use online dating sites is single seniors.[4]

When seventy-year-old Hilda Gottlieb's husband

passed away six years ago, she was determined not to let her loss get the best of her. So she turned to online dating.

"I was 64 when my husband died, and I knew I was not going to be alone for the rest of my life," Gottlieb told the *Palm Beach Post*.[5]

Gottlieb stumbled upon the profile of then-seventy-two-year-old Marv Cohen and decided to e-mail him. That e-mail led to an in-person meeting and an eventual romantic relationship. They have been enjoying doing things together ever since.

The point is that online dating these days is viewed as socially acceptable even among many of the people who were perhaps the most suspicious of it a few short years ago.

Online Dating Is Now Hypermainstream

"The stigma [of online dating] has definitely dropped because people are advocating for it, talking with their friends [about it], sharing stories with families," says Lija Jarvis, director of a large survey study on Internet dating.[6] Another study, conducted by the research firm Chadwick Martin Bailey, shows how quickly online dating—in existence for less than two decades—has revolutionized the way people find and pursue potential mates.

"It does seem to have displaced all other forms of dating," says Susan Frohlick, a cultural anthropologist at the University of Manitoba who has studied online dating. "I would say that it's been in the last five years that it's become hypermainstream."[7]

So if you are embarrassed by a passé prejudice against online dating, do your best to move beyond it. Swallow your irrational pride, and the outdated stigma you're holding on to will disappear.

Remember This

Any remaining stigma about online dating you may still hold is only going to weigh you down in this process. So here are some tips for getting beyond it.

Talk to fellow cyberdaters: If you think that dating online means you're doing something reprehensible—something that's simply not done—you need to talk with some of the millions of others who are doing it. The more you talk to others who are dating online, the more you will see how normal it can be.

Talk to some dot-com-dating success stories: Just as talking to some online daters may help you see this process for what it is, so will talking with some couples who have found their soul mates online. You'll find them in any church. Just ask around. Nearly everyone knows someone who has gotten married as a result of meeting online. Ask some of these people how the process was for them. If they are like most online matches, they will be thrilled to tell you their stories and relate their experiences.

Check out online dating books: If you need further evidence of how mainstream cyberdating is, peruse the relationship section of any major bookstore. You'll see countless books on finding online love. In fact, there are so many that some are even directed toward specific groups, such as baby boomers or widows and so on.

2
Myth: Dating Online Means You're Desperate

It is characteristic of wisdom not to do desperate things.

—HENRY DAVID THOREAU

AFTER YEARS OF SINGLEDOM, Doug Broxson tried online dating on a whim. And that's when he met Pat Montesino. She was a skeptic of online dating too. He was sure he wouldn't remarry after the death of his wife. Yet when he met Pat, they found they had much in common. They sensed an immediate connection even on their first date, and in time, Doug asked Pat to do something that had once seemed unimaginable to him: He asked Pat to marry him. "I thought I was happy by myself, until I met Pat. Then I knew what happy was, living in paradise with my best friend," says Doug.[1]

Countless stories like this one are told every day about singles who were reluctant to try online dating. They may have had a myriad of reasons, but one of the most common is that they thought going online would mean they were desperate. But nothing could be further from the truth. Going online to find your soul mate doesn't mean you've run out of other options; it means you're being smart about looking for love.

Consider Julie, thirty-one. She was slow to get online but was convinced once one of her close friends found the love of her life through a dating site. "I've been online for just three weeks so far. I have been getting approximately six matches a day, and I generally get contacted by two or three of those guys. But I'm taking my time. I'm in no rush," says Julie. "I've been on two in-person dates. Both men were genuinely nice guys, but I haven't had any real chemistry with anyone yet." She's obviously not desperate. She's just being smart. "I'm taking this approach," she says: "Keep 'em coming! One guy down, another guy closer to my dream man."

"Please Love Me"

We've all seen the overeager attitude, clingy behavior, and crazy intonations that cry out, *Please love me!*

And nobody finds that attractive. But if you think all the millions of singles who are online have this unappealing attitude, you're simply mistaken. Sure, there are desperate online daters, just as there are desperate daters in traditional settings.

You know the type: always fishing for compliments, afraid of getting dumped, and in constant need of a relationship update ("What's going on between us?"). Desperate dates will also tolerate poor treatment in a relationship and make excuses for their partners' gruffness or unhealthy habits. Why? Because they can't stand the thought of not being needed. It all comes down to personal insecurity. And that can be found both online and offline. It has nothing to do with trying to find your right someone through a dating site.

In fact, desperate daters are typically people who quickly dial down their standards and accept almost anyone in place of no one. They compromise their beliefs and try to convince themselves that they like certain qualities they really don't. Online dating diminishes these tendencies because it matches people on the basis of what they have previously expressed liking. So we could easily argue that, on reputable dating sites, people are likely to find the most secure and nondesperate daters in the singledom.

Carl, an online dater in his mid-thirties, says it well: "Meeting online through a dating site is no different from meeting at a party or at a restaurant or at church. Once you've met, it's real life. You either fall for each other, or you don't. You either have a great connection, or you don't." Carl goes on to say, "It's not like using your computer to find the person of your dreams is a sign that you're desperate. It's just another way to put yourself in a position to meet somebody that might be a great match."

Remember This

Let's face facts. If you're a little over-amped for finding the right someone, if you're feeling a bit desperate in your dating life, you're bound to come off desperate when you're dot-com dating too. We understand. You want love. You really, really want love. Desperately. You're not alone. Almost anyone who has been single for an extended period of time knows the pain that comes from wanting to be in a relationship and not being able to make it happen. But desperation is never attractive.

And here's what you may not realize: The more you want love, the more desperate you feel; the more desperate you feel, the needier you appear; the needier you appear, the less attractive you become to a potential mate. So consider the following tips for curbing your desperation:

Recognize where the "neediness" comes from: Your neediness stems from feeling deprived or disadvantaged. You feel needy because you're holding on to an irrational thought that says all the good ones are taken or you're missing your window for love. But this is simply not true. People find love at every age and stage. And online dating only increases the odds of your finding what you're after. So stop thinking of yourself as deprived of love and instead see how you now have an abundance of opportunities to find it. This may sound simple, but this attitudinal shift will change your whole countenance—and keep neediness at bay.

Move slowly: When you do meet someone who sparks your interest, take things slowly. Don't be in a hurry to rush the relationship. Let it unfold and take a natural course. Relationships have various levels of connection, and if you try to skip through any of them prematurely, you're bound not only to miss out on the sweetness of the journey but also to scare off the person you thought held such promise.

Lean into God's love: We know. You've heard this sermon before. But it's worth repeating. The healthiest people on this planet are those who find their identities firmly rooted in God's grace. They're not working to earn it. They know and feel God's love, and as a result, it radiates from them. To paraphrase St. Augustine, God loves you as if you were the only person on the planet to love. Keep that in mind. Meditate on God's love for you until you experience it deep in your soul. Once you do, your desperation will dissipate.

3

Myth: Free Online Dating Sites Are the Best Bargains

If you pay peanuts, you get monkeys.

—JAMES GOLDSMITH

LET'S FACE IT. Our culture is enamored with bargains. The desire to get "more for less" permeates our economy. And it pays off for some. Just ask Wal-Mart or IKEA. And we're even more attracted to "free." Even wealthy celebrities can't resist getting something for nothing. Between the red carpet and the Grammy or Golden Globe stage, for example, they find their goodies in a "gifting lounge," where they are lavished with all sorts of freebies. And the likes of Gwyneth Paltrow and Brad Pitt eat it up. Everyone, even rich people, likes "free."

17

So why not go the free route when it comes to online dating? As Christine, thirty-seven, asked us, "Why in the world would anyone in their right mind pay for an online dating service when you can get the same thing for free?" That's a valid question. And to answer Christine, we could simply respond, "You can't." But allow us to elaborate on that with four reasons that will explain why you can't get the same thing for free.

Are You for Real?

First and foremost, free sites typically have no identity-verification system in place. This means that if and when you make contact with someone, you have no realistic guarantee that you are talking to the person you think you are. On free sites it's easy for people to be imposters—not just providing misleading information about themselves but completely fabricating who they are.

Why would people do this? Bogus profiles and phony identities are used in all kinds of scams to prey on potential online daters. For example, a user can spam a free site with fake profiles that are in reality advertisements for other services, such as prostitution, multilevel marketing, or other personals Web sites.

Not only that, but free sites can often attract married people who like the idea of chatting it up, fooling around, and having affairs with single people. Whatever the motive, this can obviously be an unnerving aspect of pursuing a match on a free site, because even when members' profiles are "real," there is still an inherent lack of trust among other members.

Is Anybody Home?

Second, since users of free sites often sign up on impulse and have little or nothing invested in their online dating experience, they frequently never return to the site to follow up. Unlike a more reputable site where users are paying for the service, free users are simply not as committed to the online experience. People on a paid site are far more likely to be serious about wanting to actually find someone, and therefore, they will actively use the site.

Since they didn't sign up on a whim (like some users on free sites), paying users are invested in actually using the service they paid for. But a majority of free dating sites keep profiles online for months or even years after the last time the person logged in, thereby making it seem that there are more available members than there actually are. If a paid site attempts to do this, that fact will eventually become known and will tarnish the site's reputation.

Time Is Money, Right?

Third, paid sites are more time efficient. Because free sites typically make their money from streaming ads, the user experience is not as clean and easy. As one user we know says, "A free site is like going to a free movie theater but being interrupted every five minutes during the movie."

Quantity or Quality?

Fourth, the quality of members is typically better on a paid site. Why? Because once you are required to use your credit card for the service, you immediately eliminate a lot of the "undesirables" and scammers who either troll the free sites misrepresenting themselves or only sign up on a whim. You also eliminate the likelihood of "serial daters" who are not looking for a serious relationship. Free sites are generally about the proverbial hookup. So if you're looking for love instead of a fling, your chances of finding it on a free site are significantly lower.

The right paid sites are as invested in helping you find a serious relationship as you are in finding one.

They spend a great deal of time and money to keep scammers and people who aren't serious from being on their sites. They are highly motivated to keep their sites credible and reputable among their users. If they fail at this, they go out of business. But free sites want to bring in as many users as possible— regardless of their character qualities. That's why paid sites also invest more in customer service than free sites. One more thing: Paid sites would never sell your information to third parties as some free sites do. It's widely known in the industry that free sites sometimes harvest users' personal information and contacts to use in e-mail spam.[1]

The Cost of a Free Site

The bottom line is that when it comes to the services and the outcomes of online dating, you get what you pay for. If you are interested in finding a serious and trustworthy relationship (as opposed to short-term "casual dating" or hookups), your chances of finding it on a free site, when compared to a reputable fee-based site, are dramatically diminished. And when you add to that the idea of finding not only a serious relationship but also a relationship with someone who shares your heartfelt Christian values and life-style, your chances diminish even further.

The appeal of a "free" Internet dating service is obvious—it's free. But that's exactly where the appeal generally ends.

Remember This

Most popular does not always equal best: The fact that a lot of people use an online site that is free doesn't mean that site is a good bargain. Do you really want your dates from your online site to be the same types of people you meet casually every week? "Free" often suggests a low level of investment, both emotionally and financially, from the people you are meeting on that site. That is why it is worth the effort and investment to investigate the right type of online dating experience for you and to find matches who truly line up with your own personality, interests, and values. In addition, the answers to the following two questions can help you to make a wise decision when choosing an online site.

How much should you spend on dating online? The amount spent annually by individual users of online matching sites is approximately $280, with an average cost of about $30 per month. The reason for the difference in the amounts is that users can purchase the service by the month (the most expensive way, where the cost may be as much as $60 per month) or by the year (which is the best value). Of course, there is a wide spectrum of price structures, and sites also offer specials from time to time.[2]

Is there a time when you need to reevaluate your investment? People sometimes give up too early on a dating site because they don't think enough is happening. Our advice to these people is to "work" the site. You can't expect it to deliver a dream date to your doorstep just because you're a member of the site. You've got to invest time in using the tools the site provides for making the best connections possible. The time to reevaluate is when, after giving a site a chance, you realize that the other members on the site are not consistent with what you are seeking. In other words, if the site is populated with the kinds of people you don't want to date, it's time to move on. But generally speaking, if the site has a good pool of prospects and you're just not finding your right someone yet, hang in there. Some people find their right match quickly, and others seem to take time—just as in the real world of dating.

4
Myth: Only Liars, Losers, and Freaks Are on Dating Sites

The hardest tumble a man can make is to fall over his own bluff.

—AMBROSE BIERCE

SANDRA MET A MAN through a dating site the summer before she began grad school. "Mike seemed like a nice Christian guy. We had great conversations online, and we clicked over the phone," she says. "So I met him at an Italian restaurant for a meal. He resembled his online photos, but his demeanor and social style were off. All he wanted to talk about was theology." Sandra explained that she'd never heard of some of the words he was using. "He wasn't like this online, so it was really weird. And he wanted to show how superior he was to me. When he talked about taking me to see his collection of theology books at his apartment, I called it quits and headed home."

James, an athletic guy in his early forties, met Tiffany in person after more than three months of connecting through a free dating site. He thought they had a lot in common, and he loved the way Tiffany looked in her photos, especially the one where she was playing tennis. They exchanged friendly banter via e-mail and talked on the phone several times. By the time they scheduled their in-person date, James couldn't have been more excited. They met at a public tennis court for a friendly volley. But when Tiffany showed up, James knew something was wrong. Not only did she not bring a tennis racquet, but she didn't bring her true identity. "You really look different from your photos," James said with genuine surprise. Tiffany said something about being out of shape after a car accident that happened four years ago. But it wasn't just that she weighed far more than her photos depicted; her face did not resemble the face in her photos. James called the match before they even stepped on the court.

Unfortunately, these kinds of encounters do happen—in real-world dating as well as online. But they aren't typical; they are the result of a minority of online daters who either create misleading online profiles or who are simply socially inept.

Online Dating Is the Same as Real-World Dating

When you look for a date online, you learn a lot more about potential dates than you would if they were just people your great-aunt kept setting you up with. On the other hand, you lack the advantage of knowing the person's history. Years ago, you might have dated a girl you knew from college or the guy from down the street. You would have had some window into their backgrounds, and they would have had some window into yours. But Internet dating lacks that kind of social history, which is why some people occasionally encounter wackos who misrepresent themselves or are simply strange.

Generally, people who lie on online dating sites "are people-pleasers who want to present themselves in the most favorable light to get someone to like them—just as they would in face-to-face dating."[1] In fact, studies have found that while online daters round off the sharp edges of truth when it comes to height, weight, and age, the deceptions are usually small.[2]

Jeffrey Hall, of the University of Kansas, surveyed more than five thousand Internet matching-service participants in an attempt to find out what kinds of people are most likely to lie when dating online. He asked them how likely they were to lie about various topics, including relationship goals, personal attributes, age, weight, etc.

He found that when it comes to gender differences, women tend to tell white lies about their weight. Men tend to fib about their past relationships. However, Hall and his team concluded that men and women behave the same online as they would if introduced face-to-face, dispelling the myth that people are more dishonest when going online to meet others. In fact, if people (irrespective of gender) are going to lie, it doesn't matter whether they are online or not.[3]

Looking for Short, Fat, Bald, and between Jobs?

"What people lie about really depends on the type of people they are," says Hall. "Someone who is really open to new experiences, likes going hiking in the mountains, likes to go travel to foreign countries—they are very unlikely to misrepresent themselves based upon their interests because they are very interesting people. A more open person would be very unlikely to lie about what they are interested in because they are interested in many things."[4] On the other hand, an introverted person may "invent" some interests simply to seem a bit more interesting. In other words, when people misrepresent themselves on these sites, they do so because they want to be liked. No big surprise, right? If you're wanting to be attractive to others, you probably don't lead your profile with, "I'm short, fat, and bald."

But what *may be* surprising if you think that online sites are only for freaks or losers is Hall's conclusion: "Online daters shouldn't be concerned that most people are presenting a false impression of themselves. What influences face-to-face dating influences the online world, too." In other words, when it comes to misleading a potential date and unusual interactions, online dating is no different than traditional dating.[5]

Remember This

With everyone you meet online, you need to ask yourself whether there is any reason to be especially cautious or concerned. If for any reason connecting with another person doesn't feel right, trust that instinct. Don't dismiss it as insignificant. It's telling you something, so pay close attention to it. Here are some specific signs that should always raise a red flag:

Negative comments: Any name-calling or blaming is cause for concern, such as referring to someone as a "loser." Why? Because it is a pretty reliable indicator of a lack of responsibility. In other words, when people are posting negative comments on their profiles, they are likely to be the kinds of people who are shirking accountability or, at the very least, lacking an acceptable standard for conscientiousness. So move on.

Arrogance: Everyone has an inner radar related to conceit. If your radar meter is going off after reading a profile or communicating with an online date, keep moving. Who wants to be with people who are full of themselves, always wanting to impress others with the kinds of cars they drive or the awards they've won? That one-way conversation gets old fast. And it's likely to be the tip of an unhealthy iceberg. Being self-absorbed is a sure sign of a lack of empathy. And empathy—the capacity to put yourself in someone else's shoes—is critical to any meaningful relationship.

Inconsistency: If you notice that portions of people's profiles seem out of character with the rest of their profiles, or if their communication doesn't match their profiles, it's a good sign that there are problems ahead. It could mean that those people are struggling with emotional problems or with drugs or alcohol. It could mean that they have other people communicating for them. And who wants that?

Instant attachment: Getting attached too quickly is another cause for concern. If the people you're communicating with are overeager to meet or if they express a feeling, early on, that they already know you, beware. These are signs that those individuals are controlling or are feeling very empty and insecure. They may flatter you with complimentary messages, but don't be fooled by their neediness. It's not healthy. So, once again, run!

5

Myth: Online Dating Takes the Romance out of the Dating Experience

For some reason, Christians are taught to be diligent and responsible in every area of their life except dating.

—HENRY CLOUD

ALLOW US TO GIVE you a quick quiz. Answer these half-dozen questions with your first impulse. There's no need to give them serious consideration.

- True or False: Love is an indescribable feeling that overwhelms you.
- True or False: True love is blind.
- True or False: Falling in love just happens—you can't plan it.
- True or False: I believe in love at first sight.
- True or False: If you trust your heart, you'll eventually find love when you least expect it.
- True or False: Love has its own reasons that you often can't explain.

If you answered "true" to most of these items, most people probably consider you a romantic. That is, you're often guided more by feelings than by facts. You're more sentimental than practical. More dramatic than demure. And chances are that you tend to buy into the myth that says online dating steals the romance from the relationship.

You might be like Randy, thirty-four, a copy editor for a regional magazine. "Call me old-fashioned," he says, "but when it comes to meeting the love of your life, I'd like it to be somewhere other than sitting at my computer keyboard. That seems too detached and clinical." He goes on to say, "I still have this ideal that two strangers can meet each other's gaze across a crowded room while the world melts away."

Do you identify with Randy? If so, we don't want to argue with you, but allow us to make a case for why online dating *doesn't* take the romance out of the experience.

Romance Is All about the Feelings

Titanic. Casablanca. When Harry Met Sally. West Side Story. Beauty and the Beast. Sleepless in Seattle. Jerry Maguire. The list of popular romantic movies could easily fill several pages. And what do all these romantic tales have in common? They are all love stories that evoke some of the deepest emotions within the human heart.

Anything wrong with that? Of course not. The problem arises when we begin to base our searches for love—whether using the Internet or more traditional means—on replicating these feelings. In other words, when we buy into the idea that it's how we *feel* in our hearts that matters most, we become misguided in our searches for the right someone. In fact, when this kind of emotion becomes the overriding guideline for identifying potential mates, we discount the objective basis for finding partners.

Emotions are often unreliable. While they serve an important function in the process, they are biased, whimsical, and at times, tyrannical. They can be manipulated by hormones. They can be distorted by unconscious desires that go back even as far as unmet needs from childhood (paging Dr. Freud?). They lie to us as often as they tell us the truth. When people "follow their hearts" without using their heads to find true love, they're likely to eventually end up with broken hearts.

True love, the kind that goes the distance and matures over time—the kind that helps two people become better together than they would be apart—is the result of a balancing act between the head and the heart. True love results from balancing an objective approach with emotional yearnings or, in other words, from balancing thinking with feeling.

Online Dating Can Be Your Balance Beam

One of the great advantages to becoming an online dater is that if you are using the right site, you will have an automatic means for balancing your head and your heart. Why? Because the right site helps you hone your thinking from the start—before your heart can get swept away in a sea of swirling emotions.

You begin rather rationally, by carefully considering what you know you need if you are to build a relationship that will last a lifetime. You note your preferences and even your standards. For example, if you know that for your relationship to have a fighting chance your partner needs to share your Christian values and your lifestyle choices, the site you choose to use can ensure that you will not even be *tempted* to adjust these important standards because it won't tempt you with choices that don't include them. And this gives your heart more freedom in the process.

You might say that dating online allows your romantic side to flourish. Because the site can serve as a safeguard against unhealthy compromise, your heart can be freer than ever. The right dating site automatically keeps your head and heart working together—even if you aren't conscious of it.

Online Dating Is a Quicker Means to Romance

Do you still think that online dating takes the romance out of the process? If so, we want to make one more simple point that you might be missing. After reviewing all your potential matches, after a bit of online communication, perhaps some flirtatious exchanges, and a few phone calls, you'll eventually schedule a face-to-face meeting. Now, if you don't have the traditional butterfly feelings you'd have in going out on any first date, you're not a romantic to begin with. The point is that online dating is merely a prelude to getting you connected in real life with the person that just might sweep you off your feet.

Remember This

Online dating is no less romantic than any other fix-up courtesy of your aunt or a coworker or anyone else. True romance happens when a spark occurs between two people—regardless of how they meet.

If you are having trouble imagining romance online, consider watching *You've Got Mail* again. It was filmed in 1998, when AOL was still the craze. Even so, Tom Hanks and Meg Ryan will give you a good idea of what romance looks like online. With this in mind, here are a few tips for finding that special spark online:

Short notes: The best way to see whether there is a spark is to keep your online notes short (and sweet). What you want to do is establish a back-and-forth pattern to see if you click with a person. Do you get each other? Do you both find the same things funny?

Mystery: One of the elements of romance is mystery—in this case, what is left unsaid and what can be read between the lines. Writing a ten-page introduction about yourself is one of the fastest ways to kill any romantic feelings on the recipient's part (and is a big online faux pas as well).

The extras: When you are trying to find your right someone online, it's the wrong time to be efficient. Spend time on the extras in life—smelling the flowers, taking in the view, lingering over coffee. What is the one "extra" in life you yearn to experience fully? Talk about that online, and invite your date to experience it with you. Sharing an invigorating, life-affirming experience with someone special is one of the best ways to discover the spark.

Ambience: Setting does contribute to a romantic mood. Think about it. Movie scenes tend to linger on a couple's first encounter to capture the love-at-first-sight moment, usually in a romantic location— a city park, a busy shopping district in a city, a dimly lit café, a bookstore. Even if a fast-food restaurant is conveniently located halfway between the two of you, don't agree to meet there for a first date. Instead, meet at a park, a beach, a museum, an outdoor café, a bookstore, a library—someplace that has more ambience and less fluorescent lighting.

6

Myth: Online Dating Goes against God's Guidance

Many Christians take the superspiritual approach in their
quest for a soul mate by expecting God to play the
cosmic matchmaker.

—PASTOR BEN YOUNG

BRYCE, A THIRTY-NINE-YEAR-OLD single stockbroker is one of the most sincere Christians we know. He's devoted in his faith and eager to find a woman who shares his heartfelt values. "I never thought I'd still be single at this stage of my life," Bryce says, "but I know that God has a plan, and I'm just trying to live in his timing."

Some of his friends have encouraged Bryce to try an online dating site for Christians, but Bryce has his doubts. "I'm not sure that it's something I should do," he confides to his pastor. "I mean, if I sign up for a dating site and pay a company to help me find my future wife, doesn't it mean I'm not trusting God to do that for me?"

"That's a good question, Bryce," his pastor responds. "But nowhere in the Bible does it say, 'Thou shalt not use the Internet to find your spouse.'"

"I know," Bryce says with a smile, "but this is such an important part of my life, and it seems that God would want me to trust *him*, not my computer, to find the woman he wants me to marry."

"Maybe so," his wise pastor continues, "but maybe God also wants you to use this tool to help you do just that. Maybe the woman he has in mind for you is looking for you online already."

"Do you think so?"

"I don't know, but I have a tough time believing that it's not Christian to use the Internet to find your spouse. If you were looking for a job, Bryce, you'd want to trust God in the process but still do everything you could, including using the Internet, to help you."

What about you? We assume that you're a committed Christian (or you probably wouldn't be reading this book). Do you have the same sentiment as Bryce? Do you wonder whether God would want you to use online dating or not? Do you fear that using the Internet to find your right someone would mean that you're not trusting God?

Seeking God's Will for Your Love Life

Let's start with the fundamentals. As a Christian, you want God's leading for your life—you want to avoid making a decision that goes against his will. Theologian Garry Friesen outlines four debilitating traps that ensnare even sincere Christians who are a bit naive about finding God's will on important decisions, such as how to find their future spouses. Consider each one:

1. Justifying an unwise decision on the ground that "God told me to do it."
2. Fostering costly delays in the process because of uncertainty about God's will.
3. The practice of "Putting out a fleece"—allowing circumstances to dictate the decision.
4. Rejecting personal preferences when faced with apparently equal options.[1]

If you were to select the one item from this list that you might be prone to do in following God's will for your life, which one would it be? Now explore how it might hinder your thinking about online dating. Are you tempted to put out a fleece? For example, does God need to bring you "the one" within one month of online dating? Or do you think online dating is against God's will for you because it's something you'd actually prefer to do? As you apply these debilitating traps to your thinking about online dating, you may see just how naive they are.

The bottom line is that the Bible nowhere forbids online dating, and therefore, neither should we. There's no need for guilt. We don't want to make the mistake the Pharisees did and invent "sins" that weren't mentioned in the Bible.

What Matters Is Your Motivation

If you are using online dating to find a God-honoring person to date and eventually marry, your motivations are in line with Christian standards. That's pretty obvious, and it's bound to bring God pleasure. But Scripture often urges us to carefully *examine* our motives (see Jeremiah 17:9; Luke 6:43-45; James 1:14), so let's go a bit deeper.

When it comes to online dating, there's a subtle motivator that can creep into the process almost without your noticing. It's a motivation to take the steering wheel of your life out of God's hands. It happens when you feel hopeless about God's provision and timing in giving you a spouse. In other words, you may have an underlying motive that says, *I don't trust God anymore in this area, and I'm taking matters into my own hands.* If that's the case, of course, your motivation needs some careful reexamination. We're certainly not saying that you shouldn't be proactive in pursuing the prospect of marriage in your life. Far from it. But we are suggesting that you consider any unhealthy motivations that push God out of the process. This is just as true in traditional dating matters, by the way, as it is for the online approach.

As long as you're motivated to let God direct your steps, even in the online dating process, and to follow his will as he reveals it to you, you'll make decisions that honor him. Of course, this means taking time for daily prayer and meditation on God's Word. It means routinely evaluating your motives in calm, nonpressured moments. It means acknowledging the Holy Spirit's direction in your life. It also means seeking the counsel of wise Christians you respect who can speak truth into your life and give you feedback on any decisions you're contemplating.

The Best Way to Keep Online Dating Holy

Perhaps the biggest danger of online dating for Christians is that it can become a solitary act. That is, it can occur in isolation. As Christians, we are called to live in community (see Proverbs 15:22;

24:6; Hebrews 3:12-13; 10:24-25). And for good reason. We need the fellowship and guidance of other believers who can offer wisdom about our situation—and that includes something as important as looking for love online. You need people who know you and care about you to walk with you through the process.

This is one of the best ways to ensure that your decision-making standards remain high and that your motivations are honoring to God. For this reason we believe it's generally a good idea to invite family or trusted friends into the experience with you so you have people with whom to talk through your decisions. Of course, this is a personal thing, so we're not suggesting you broadcast it or that you delineate every detail. We're simply saying that having a small community of support as you pursue online dating is a great way to be sure you stay in God's will. This is particularly important as your online exchanges evolve into in-person dates. Bringing your new dates into your Christian community is vital to nurturing a relationship that honors God.

Remember This

If you're feeling at all uneasy about using an online matching site to find the love of your life because you think that it may not agree with your Christian faith, consider the following suggestions:

Pray for guidance: As you explore the idea of online dating—and even if you're already using it—ask God to guide you in the process. Ask for discernment and help at dating wisely; ask for ears to hear a person's heart rather than being distracted by superficial qualities. Surround the experience in prayer by seeking wisdom along the way.

Talk with Christian friends: If you are in a small group at your church, for example, bring up the topic of dot-com dating, and ask others to weigh in on it. If you're feeling emotionally safe, ask them to speak into your own life as you explore the idea of finding love online. They know your personality and may see things you're not aware of that can be helpful to you in the process.

Read relationship books by godly authors: The more you educate yourself on what others are saying not only about online dating as a Christian but also dating and relationships in general in the Christian faith, the wiser you will become. As you probably know, there are dozens of great relationship books by respected Christian authors to choose from.

Consult your minister: If you are particularly uncertain about whether there is a place in your faith walk for using an online dating site, you may want to meet with someone on your church's ministerial staff. Let that person know what's on your mind, and ask him or her to pray for you and to offer guidance.

Part 2

Six Ways to Know Whether Online Dating Is for You

To know how to
use knowledge is
to have wisdom.
—CHARLES SPURGEON

7

Online Dating Is for You . . . If You're Tired of Waiting for Love to Find You

Too many people go through life waiting for things to happen instead of making them happen.

—SASHA AZEVEDO

IN THE AUTUMN OF 1992, we did something unusual. We offered a course at Seattle Pacific University that promised to openly and honestly answer questions about relationships. We called it Relationships 101, and since it was to be a general elective, required for no one, we worried that students at this Christian university might not sign up.

We couldn't have been more wrong. Since that first semester, we've had an annual waiting list of students who are eager to get into the jam-packed auditorium and learn about everything from friendship to family, from sexuality to gender. And, of course, dating, especially a lecture we call "How to Fall in Love without Losing Your Mind."

From the course's inception we have made it a tradition to begin each session by having a student choose a song that relates to that day's topic. We're never sure what we'll hear, but a popular song is always a quick and easy way to get the students interested in the day's subject.

On one occasion, when the topic was dating, we walked into the lecture hall of more than two hundred students and soon heard an increasingly heavy beat coming from the large auditorium speakers. The students' chatter diminished as the room filled with the rhythm, followed by the familiar voice of Bono:

> *I have climbed highest mountains*
> *I have run through the fields*
> *Only to be with you*
> *Only to be with you.*

The class immediately recognized the U2 tune and laughed uproariously as they mentally connected the song's lyrics with dating. And as Bono got to the chorus, they sang in unison:

> *But I still haven't found what I'm looking for.*

That's when the students began cheering. They couldn't contain their emotions. They literally whooped and hollered, nodding their heads at each other and giving the proverbial thumbs-up to the student who had selected the day's song.

That response says something, don't you think? Even college students, in their dating prime with thousands of peers and potential dating partners walking around campus, are commiserating with one another about not being able to find the right someone.

Are You Finding What You're Looking For?

Of course, you don't have to be in college to know this feeling. In reality, the emotional longing only intensifies over time for most single adults. When you're not any closer to finding a date worth keeping, each year that rolls by can make your heart ache all the more—whether you have never been married or you have a relationship history that's left you with an already fragile heart. One indicator of this becomes evident in a recent Australian study that found the biggest group of online daters are those who have been single for five or more years (38.4 percent), followed by those who have been single for one to two years (26.7 percent).[1] The point is

that waiting for love can truly try your patience—
and that's why online dating becomes so valuable.
Regardless of your age or stage, it puts an end to the
passive process of waiting.

For many single people there comes a point when
the customary dating scene just doesn't seem to cut
it. They've cycled through various church groups,
hung out at notable hot spots, participated in group
activities for singles of their age, and probably been
set up by friends or family for more than one disap-
pointing date. Does this describe you? Are you getting tired of waiting for love to find you?

If you're growing weary of waiting to find your
right someone, you don't have to keep waiting.
Online dating has little to do with waiting. It puts
you in the driver's seat, helping you to be proactive
about the fate of your dating life. You don't have to
sit home alone on Friday nights. And you don't have
to date duds just because your options are drying up.
Online dating can broaden your prospects and help
you find the someone you've been looking for.

Online Dating Puts a Light at the End of the "Single" Tunnel

Ben, thirty-nine, has been looking for love longer
than he wants to admit. Truth be told, he thought

he'd be married shortly after graduating from college. But when he landed his dream job, repping for a major sports-equipment company, he became consumed by it. In fact, Ben climbed the proverbial corporate ladder quickly. He was traveling nonstop and loving it. But he *wasn't* loving the fact that he hadn't found his right someone. He'd dated here and there, even going to various singles events at different churches to find prospects, but nothing was clicking.

On a whim, Ben tried online dating. And that's where he found Jennifer. She wasn't the first match that came his way, of course. He explored several potential connections before he discovered the match with Jennifer. But that was all it took. She lived about two hours away, but as he eventually said, they became the shortest two hours of his life. "I can't imagine living without her," he said as a newlywed. "And to think I might have missed out on ever meeting Jen if I hadn't got fed up with waiting and eventually gone online."

Cindi is another example. "I can't believe I'm in my forties and in this situation," she blurted out. "If I'm ever going to have children, I need to find someone soon." In her twenties, Cindi married a guy she met in college. Three years later, after he revealed that he was in love with another woman, the marriage was over. A few years after that excruciating chapter of her life (and after working hard to rebuild some trust issues), Cindi decided to date once again. She even dated one guy for more than a year. But he wasn't the *right* guy. Five long years later, after the breakup of that dating relationship, Cindi decided to try online dating—something she thought she'd never do. And after hanging in there with it, that's exactly where she found her Mr. Right.

The truth is that changes in our society have made it more difficult to meet people through traditional methods. People marry later, work longer hours, have less time, and live farther from family members who might introduce them to a neighbor's handsome, eligible nephew or beautiful, single niece. That's where a mouse and a modem can step in and make all the difference between merely waiting for love and actually finding it.

Remember This

Online dating allows you to date with dignity. It takes much of the sting out of a process that is otherwise fraught with some not-so-pleasant experiences. Here are a few of the positive trade-ins that online daters gain:

Trade in high anxiety for high comfort:
You do online dating on your own
schedule, when and where you want.
There's no need to get dressed up and
plan an engaging activity just to see if
sparks might fly. You can set the wheels
in motion while sitting in your own home,
wearing sweats, and sipping coffee.

Trade in rejection for selection: Online
dating allows you to focus on people who
are interested in you. No, it doesn't guard
you completely from feelings of rejection,
but it's a world away from getting turned
down for a date in real life.

**Trade in being chosen for being a
chooser:** Online dating puts you in the
driver's seat. This is particularly important
for women. You no longer have to feel as
if you're sitting around passively waiting
for a guy to make the move. It's cool for
anyone to initiate contact when it comes
to online dating.

**Trade in randomness for
receptiveness:** Online dating takes
the guesswork out of potential daters'

intentions. After all, if they're on a dating site, you know they are looking for a date. You don't have to hint around to see if they are "on the market.".

8

Online Dating Is for You . . . If You Want to Instantly and Dramatically Increase Your Chances for Love

You've heard it before, "All the good ones are taken!" The way people talk, you would think that mates were an extinct species.

—EDWARD A. DREYFUS

"ALL THE GOOD ONES ARE TAKEN," Jennifer complained. "There's nobody to date—even if I lower my standards. I mean, it's not like I'm looking for a guy to ride in on a white horse and sweep me off my feet. I'd just like to meet a nice guy with a decent job and a sense of humor. Is that too much to ask?"

"I know what you mean," her friend Sarah commiserated. "It feels like all the guys where I work are already paired up, or they are simply not dating material. I mean, I'm not going out with a guy whose idea of a nice date is Taco Bell and video games."

"Seriously," Jennifer continued. "I don't even know if some guys think of it as a date. Three weeks ago I went on that hike with First Church, and there were some cute guys in the group. I ended up talking to one of them most of the hike, and then he asked me to have a cup of coffee with him when we got back to the church. I think he's a nice guy, but I don't even know if he considered that a date. He texted me a couple of times since, but was it just a friendly thing or what?"

This little exchange between friends is echoed in one form or another countless times among singles. In fact, it's one of the top complaints of single people: There's nobody to date.

The Truth about Your Dating Odds

Could this really be true? With ninety million singles in America, could it be that all the good ones near you are taken? That's unlikely. According to the American Association for Single People, an "unmarried majority" has emerged in most major cities, as well as in several states. In fact, nearly a majority of households in the nation are headed by unmarried adults.[1] So why is it that singles are complaining about not finding anyone to date?

In fact, let's make this more personal. Consider

your situation. If you were to make a list of all the potential people to date in your social circles right now, how long would it be? Can you list a dozen eligible people you'd consider dating, or a half dozen? Or would you, like most single adults, have a tough time coming up with a significant list of potential people to date?

The problem, of course, is not that there are no other compatible, attractive, interesting, fun, and successful singles to date—they are more plentiful than ever. The problem is that most singles—especially Christian singles—just don't know where to find them. After "shopping" various church groups and attending events with like-minded Christians, where do you go? Of course, some singles "hook up" at local bars on a routine basis. And some would point to that kind of a scene for finding other singles. But that's not what we're talking about—and neither are you. The focus here is on finding a "certain someone" to date who shares your Christian values and who could possibly even be "the one."

That's where dot-com dating comes in. Never before have members of the singles community had such an effective and powerful tool for increasing their chances of finding serious romantic matches—people who are highly compatible and potential "keepers."

A Dozen Dates in the Same Room?

Think of it this way: What if within the next twenty-four hours you could be in a room with a dozen or so eligible and compatible singles of the opposite sex? And what if you could meet with each of them one-on-one? These would be people who not only share your personal faith but who also have a great deal in common with you personally.

And what if you were to easily interact with each one of the single people in this room to learn a bit about who they are—not just their preferences but also their personalities? You could explore, for example, how you share a sense of humor. And what if you knew that all these people were just as interested as you are in finding a person to date? No sleuthing or guesswork involved. They wouldn't be in this room if they weren't looking for love.

Would you be interested in finding a room like this? If you're like most, you would. What single person wouldn't? Entering this room would instantly and dramatically increase your chances for finding a date worth keeping. And that's exactly what Internet dating does for you and your love life. Let's say this straight: Your chances of meeting compatible singles are hugely increased when you date online.

Why is this? Because a competent online dating

site virtually brings the single population to you. Your heart is no longer on a scavenger hunt. You simply consider the various options that are, literally, at your fingertips. Your computer keyboard is all that stands between you and a potential connection with as many matches as you'd like to consider.

Expanding Your Dating Horizons

After too much dissatisfaction and defeat with the more traditional dating route, or lack thereof, Jennifer finally gave in to dot-com dating. "I eventually realized I had little to lose and a lot to gain. Besides, I wanted to put a stop to dealing with blurred lines," she says. "I'm tired of asking, 'Are we friends, or are we dating?' Online I can do three dates a week with three different guys if I want to. In my regular life I don't think I even meet three new guys in a week, let alone a single guy that would possibly like to date me."

Jennifer also learned that online dating allows her to set her own parameters about whether she would like to consider dating someone who is outside of her hometown of Macon, Georgia. She decided that an hour-and-a-half drive to Atlanta was a small price to pay for finding the love of her life. And that's exactly where she found him. Todd, a manager of a sales team for a pharmaceutical company, had never been to Macon before he met Jennifer online. But as Jennifer says, "We got to the point where both of our cars could almost drive that stretch of Interstate 75 between our homes automatically."

The point is that whether you live in a large city or a small town, online dating allows you to expand your dating horizons—and thus your chances for finding true love. After all, there have been countless couples living across the country from each other, not to mention living across town, who never would have found each other had it not been for meeting on a dating site.

Remember This

Too many people assume that all the unspoken rules of relationships end when they go online, but that's simply not true. Act online as if you are in that virtual room with other singles. If talking too much about yourself and your own accomplishments in real life is a relationship faux pas, that doesn't change online. Here are some of the biggest dating mistakes people make—and repeat—online. Try to avoid them.

> **Mistake #1:** Talking too much about past dating relationships. Use your friends

for counseling, but be focused on the present and the future in online dating relationships.

Mistake #2: Letting yourself become a wallflower. Whether you are at a social event or online, you are there to meet the right one. Don't hold back too much. Other people need to get to know the interesting things about you—fun stories, exotic experiences, intriguing friends you have, and so on.

Mistake #3: Sending a mass e-mail (including your coworkers) announcing you've joined a dating Web site. Let's be honest. The reason you are on a dating site is because you want to meet new people. You know the people on your e-mail list. Do you really want Alvin in accounting to start asking you out online? However, if you are interested in starting an online dating relationship with someone you know, casually mention to that person that you are on an online dating site and see what happens.

Mistake #4: Using too many emoticons in your online communications. It's popular to use cryptic language online. But do weigh the disadvantages of using too many abbreviations, emoticons, misspelled words, and incomplete sentences online. Remember that written communication is the easiest for others to misinterpret. Verbal communication is better—and face-to-face communication is best. If you communicate cryptically online, others may misinterpret what you actually mean and, more importantly, your tone. Again, don't chuck relationship rules just because you are online. If your dinner dates ended every sentence giving exaggerated smiles and pointing at them, you might think your dates had some psychological issues. Some people interpret overuse of emoticons the same way.

9

Online Dating Is for You . . . If You Want to Find Your "Right" Match— a Date Worth Keeping

Your ability to choose the right kind of mate can either make you or break you.

—SAMUEL ADAMS

WE HAD JUST CONCLUDED our remarks on love and dating at a late-night church event for singles in Oklahoma City. As the crowd was leaving, one young woman made a beeline to the stage and, without introducing herself, asked, "How do I know if I've found the right person?"

We hear this question a lot. And it's a good one. The motivator behind the question, of course, is marriage.

"I've been dating a guy for almost two years," the young woman said, "and it's getting serious.

I just don't know if he's 'the one.'" She went on to tell us that her parents were divorced and she didn't want that to happen to her. Her current relationship was going well, but she wanted some reassurance. "I mean, we've all heard the statistics about marriages that don't make it," she continued, "and I don't want my marriage to end up as a statistic."

We're guessing you probably feel the same way. So how do you know who is the "right one" for you? You already know that you shouldn't marry someone who drinks too much, spends too much, works too much, or brags too much; uses drugs or engages in other illegal behavior; or is unfaithful, cruel, or dishonest. You know you don't want someone who is negative, selfish, wishy-washy, critical, or sloppy. But does eliminating a bunch of undesirable characteristics mean that you're well on your way to finding Miss or Mr. Right? Hardly.

What makes someone right for you has little to do with just making sure that person's not a jerk. The right match has to do with deeper and less-apparent qualities. These qualities are nearly impossible to identify unless you know where to look. But even when you can't put your finger on them, you can sense them. How? The relationship strikes a healthy tenor. You know you're a better person because this individual is in your life. You are both growing and maturing because you have each other. You feel a deep support and encouragement from each other, both intellectually and emotionally. The right person doesn't just make you feel the excitement of falling in love; he or she has something that transcends the initial elation of the relationship—a combination of qualities that mesh with yours for an abiding connection that has more than a fighting chance of going the distance.

One of the most comprehensive studies ever conducted on intimate relationships puts forward this bold conclusion: "Selecting a person with the right characteristics is perhaps the most important prerequisite for attaining the ideal of a close, personal relationship."[1] In other words, predicting the success or failure of an eventual marriage relationship rests heavily on the combination of the personality qualities of the two people in the relationship.

Of course, it can take months, even years, to discover what these sometimes-mysterious qualities are in combination with your own personality. Even after a marriage that didn't work out, some people still don't know what those qualities are for themselves, and so they repeat the same mistakes over and over in their love lives.

The Good News: No More Trial and Error

It's one thing to find a date, but quite another to find "the one"—that person who has complementary and compatible qualities that will bless your relationship until "death do you part." But today, more than ever, it's easier to find that right someone for you.

Online dating makes striking that right match less mysterious and relatively easy. Why? Because after having you fill out a painless personality assessment, the best dating sites use this information (as well as your preferences) to link you with the most optimal matches possible. Not all sites do so. In fact, only a small minority go to the trouble and expense of basing their matching systems on personality variables. The majority of sites simply set their users loose to fish the great sea of singles and find someone who sparks their interest. That is far from being the best way to find the right match.

The best sites are far more sophisticated. They use the science of relationships and work behind the scenes to deliver to you the matches that not only fit your preferences but also sync with your underlying personality traits. Over the past few years, social scientists have become very good at predicting which couples will succeed or fail in marriage. And many of the variables used for these amazing predictions are related to the personalities of the two people in the couple. We now know what makes a good match for true happiness and a long-lasting marriage.

It used to be that when a person asked, "How do I know if I've found the right person?" someone would respond, "You just know," or something similar. Well, you don't have to count on the mysteries of intuition if you're wondering if you're a good match. You don't have to guess. No more trial and error. If you're using a good matching site, you can know right from the start whether your personalities are going to eventually collide or fit like a glove.

Online Dating Doesn't Diminish Romance

As we write these words, we can almost see you wrinkling your nose and shaking your head. We work with enough singles to know that you may be thinking, *Okay, but that takes all the romance out of finding my right someone.* Don't fall for this myth. The "scientific stuff" does nothing to eliminate romance from the process. It all happens behind the scenes because of the online process. After you've completed your own personality assessment, you're barely aware of that "scientific stuff" because the online site is sifting through all the options for you and just bringing the very best ones to the top of your potential list.

Not only that, but the site is not going to select "the one" for you. It simply provides options. Many of them. You'll still need your heart to guide you in the process of finding *your* right one. The site simply keeps you from having to get your heart kicked around by matches that will not be successful in the long run.

Consider a brief analogy. If you were the CEO of your own company, you wouldn't hire a vice president based on the person's picture and a paragraph that he or she wrote about himself or herself. You wouldn't even be satisfied after a meeting or two with that person. You have too much at stake. This is an important decision that will determine the future of your company. You'd not only want to see the candidate's résumé, but you'd also likely want to find out about his or her personality characteristics to know how they will fit with your own. That's essential for predicting the success of your working relationship.

The same is true when it comes to a romantic partnership. If you want the relationship to go the distance, you have to have a good match. And today's relationship specialists know from research what combinations of personality traits mix best for longevity and happiness.

So why leave it to chance? With the right matching site, one that uses a state-of-the-art personality-assessment system, you can be more assured than ever of finding your right someone.

Remember This

More and more people are "using a mouse to find a spouse." In other words, online dating is not just about "hooking up." People who are serious about finding a long-lasting and healthy relationship are finding them online. Here are a few tips to keep in mind for doing just that:

Don't assume the first person you meet is the right person for you: Some singles—especially those who have not dated for a while—fall into the trap of thinking the first person they meet online is "the one." It can be a rush to find a good prospect, after all, when you haven't dated in eons. But don't get swept away by the first person who happens to catch your fancy. Take your time getting to know whether your personality clicks with someone else's.

Use a site that goes deeper than a picture and a paragraph: The professional community knows so much about the science of relationships these days. We know what ingredients go into fulfilling, lifelong love. And we know what causes some people to miss the mark. A good site will help you make the best choice possible.

Invite your friends and family to weigh in: Online dating can sometimes feel a bit isolating because you're meeting your "dates" one on one, not in a social setting where you might have friends who would normally give you some clues that you might be missing. So if things are heating up with an online match, don't waste too much time without seeing what the people in your life who know and love you think about the person.

10

Online Dating Is for You . . . If You Want to Use Your Time and Money Wisely

As every thread of gold is valuable, so is every moment of time.

—JOHN MASON

IF YOU WANT TO strike up an interesting conversation with someone, ask this question: Which would you rather have—more money or more time? Think about your own answer. If you could have one more hour per day at home or a six-thousand-dollar-a-year raise, which would you choose?

It turns out that just fewer than half of those polled would take the cash.[1] Fifty-one percent of us would rather have more free time, even if it means having less money. And 35 percent of us would rather earn more money, even if it means less free time. Apparently the rest of us can't quite make up our minds.[2]

Regardless of which direction you lean, when it comes to online dating, you'll generally be saving both.

How Online Dating Saves You Time

"One of the biggest bonuses of online dating for me," says Marcus, "is saving time." As a busy account manager at an advertising firm in Austin, Marcus, thirty-four, has been on the fast track. "I'm at the point in my life that I'm ready to settle down," he says. "I've been building my career, and I've certainly had some dates along the way, even a couple of relationships that were pretty long term, but I'm really ready to shift gears, get married, and have a family."

"Traditional dating is unbelievably time consuming," he confides. "First you have to find a woman to ask out, and then you have to find out if she's just interested in dating for fun or for keeps. That's what I love about using an online dating site that's devoted to finding a serious relationship (not a hookup); you know that all the other members share the same agenda—to find a date worth keeping."

Marcus is right. Online dating saves time by

helping you cut to the chase. You don't have to devote an evening to finding out whether your date is on the same page as you. You can tell that by reading his or her online profile. But it also saves valuable time in other ways. Consider all the couples you know (maybe you were part of one) who dated for months and months, only to find out that they were not compatible. Sure, they may have learned something about themselves in the process, but if they had been matched well at the beginning, they wouldn't have had to go through that long process, only to have it end in heartache. Of course, online dating does not guarantee that a similar scenario will not be played out with an online match, but it lowers the chances (as long as a reputable site is helping you match well). The point is that in online dating, you save time by knowing what you're getting into right from the start.

"It used to be," says Marcus, "that I would spend time getting to know a woman to figure out if there might be some chemistry between us. Of course, that meant getting ready for the date, and then a Friday or Saturday evening out to dinner or whatever." With online dating, that all changed. "Now I don't have to actually go out to discover whether there is a spark of promise in the relationship. It's a huge time-saver!"

Whether you identify with Marcus or not, we're pretty confident that time is important to you. These days, we all seem to work more hours than ever, and the time demands on our lives are enormous. That's why online dating is sure to save you time. Think of it this way: You can't date every day, especially after a long day at work—and especially if you are a single parent who needs to spend most evenings at home with small children. But later in the evening, after the kids are in bed, you may be able to sit down at the computer and communicate with other Christian singles who could potentially be the right someone for you. In other words, you're not going to have the time to go on actual dates, but you'll have the time for dot-com dating. You don't even have to do your hair or get dressed up!

How Online Dating Saves You Money

Few things are as exciting or as expensive as a new dating relationship. Singles report that the average first date costs anywhere from thirty dollars to over one hundred dollars, depending on where you live. And that's pretty standard for the dates that may follow. Eventually, couples tend to move away from nice dinners and concerts or movies and get more creative with dates that aren't as costly (like a picnic or pizza). Still, if you add up the money people spend getting to know a potential long-term date, the cost gets pretty steep, pretty fast.

"Okay, so getting to know each other a little bit online to see if we're a good match can keep me from incurring the predictable cash drain of dates," you may say, "but what about the expense of having to pay for the online service?"

That's a good question. But think about this logically. What you spend for a few months of online dating for a reputable and effective site is typically not more than the cost of the first date or two. And in that time you get to know not just one potential dating partner but dozens and dozens. If you think of it in these terms, you can quickly realize that online dating is not only reasonable, but it literally saves you money—assuming you're contributing to the expense of your dates. Even if you aren't, online dating saves you money in other ways. Traditional dating has the underlying expense of transportation and clothing (you want to look good, right?). And if you're not meeting potential dates online, you're likely spending money to be in places where you will find a romantic prospect. If you don't agree, just remember that old saying "Time is money," and there's no disputing the fact that the convenience of online dating is expedient.

You get the point. No need to belabor it. Online dating saves time and money.

Remember This

Online dating can be one of the most effective means single people have to steward their time and money. In fact, it can be incredibly economical on both fronts compared to real-world dating. Here are some tips to keep in mind as you leverage your online experience for doing just that.

Budget your online time: While online dating is a huge time-saver, some singles can become so engaged in the online dating process that they lose track of time. It can eat up time they need to keep their lives in balance. The point is to become aware of how much time you are devoting to this important process so that you remain "plugged in" to your real world, too.

Be intentional: Ask yourself what you want to get from your online dating experience and what qualities you are looking for in someone you want to meet. In other words, don't let random clicks of your mouse late at night determine your interest in someone. Know what is truly important to you. If you have trouble figuring that out, talk to a good friend, someone who has known you for a long time. Often, that person can identify your interests, priorities, and values more quickly than you can.

11

Online Dating Is for You . . . If You've Lost at Love and Are Ready to Find the Real Deal

The course of true love never did run smooth.

—WILLIAM SHAKESPEARE

THERESA KNEW SOMETHING was wrong. She and Brad had dated since their freshman year in college. Two years after graduation they still weren't engaged. Not that they hadn't talked about it. But every conversation ended the same way. Brad would say, "I'm never going to ask you to marry me if you are putting me under pressure." But after six years, Theresa had had enough. She gave Brad an ultimatum. He declined, and they went their separate ways, both brokenhearted. Two years later, they came back together and dated for two more years, but then

Brad told Theresa that marriage just wasn't for him. She was devastated: "I spent nearly a decade with him, thinking he was the man I would marry."

Jason says he felt as if his heart had been kicked across the room when Lisa uttered the four words every dating couple dreads: "We need to talk." Jason knew what was happening. In that one sentence, their three years of dating were unraveling before his eyes, and there was nothing he could do to stop it. For reasons he still can't explain, Lisa was calling it quits. And more than six months later, Jason's heart is still aching.

Rebecca never thought it would happen to her. After just two years of marriage, her husband revealed that he wanted out. He had fallen in love with a woman at work and without warning had announced to Rebecca that their marriage was over. She couldn't speak. She literally stood still, letting the unthinkable news sink in.

You've heard the stories of unrequited love. And there's a pretty good chance that you may have lived through one. A study involving more than 150 men and women found that only 2 percent had never been spurned by someone they loved or found themselves the object of romantic passion they did not reciprocate.[1] Some studies even indicate that as many as one out of five teenagers suffers depression because of a romantic breakup.[2] Teenagers! No wonder philosopher Erich Fromm wrote, "There is hardly any activity, any enterprise, which is started with such tremendous hopes and expectations, and yet, which fails so regularly, as love."[3]

It's true. Love hurts. Yet if your heart has been bruised or broken from a breakup, that doesn't mean you can't mend your heart and find love again. You may believe that love has passed you by, especially if the breakup is recent, but that's simply not true.

A Window to Your Future

Research shows that when the time is right—after letting yourself cry, after talking with good friends, after mourning the loss—the best remedy for a broken heart is to look forward, not backward to the past. That doesn't mean giving in to the proverbial "rebound" effect and falling into the arms of the first willing person to come along. It means cultivating some hope and optimism for your romantic future. And one of the most practical ways of doing that is to explore online dating. Why? Because online dating is an easy and painless way of looking toward what the future might hold for you. It allows you to go at your own pace. You are in the driver's seat of the experience, managing your own comfort level.

Lynn Thompson, thirty-eight, suffered the most traumatic blow of her life when she discovered that her husband had been unfaithful to her—numerous times with numerous women. She went into a dark cloud of despair. For months she could barely get out of bed in the morning to help her young daughter get ready for school and then to search for a job that would help her make ends meet. Lynn was depressed and she knew it. Her pastor tried to help, but both Lynn and her pastor knew she needed more serious intervention. With a referral to a good counselor, Lynn grappled with bottled-up anger and resentment she'd never expressed before. In time, she began to come out of her darkness. And with a nudge from her counselor some months later, she decided to try out an online dating site.

"At first, I couldn't even believe I was doing it," she confessed. "I felt like I shouldn't be there for some reason. But after a little while I began to find a part of me that I thought had been lost. I began to think about my future in a new and more positive way." The very act of opening her laptop to check out who had expressed an interest in connecting became exciting. "It's a real ego boost, after what I've been through, to see that there are decent men who might be interested in me. I've even met a couple of guys in person, and while we had fun, I'm still looking,"

Lynn says. "I now know that my right someone is out there. We're just waiting to find each other."

Who Are You Waiting to Find?

Online dating isn't a magic cure for a broken heart. But it can be a great help in the healing process. So if you've been down in the dumps for too long because love has kicked you in the teeth, we encourage you to give online dating—with a reputable site—serious consideration. The very process of going online to consider what "might be" can be scary. We know that. But it can also help you open a window to your own romantic future as you look for the person who just may be looking for you.

Remember This

If you are mending a broken heart, make sure you're in a good place emotionally before you jump into dot-com dating. When you are ready, you'll soon see what a great gift it can be for you. But the key is to ensure that you are in that good place. Here are some tips for helping you along in the healing process:

> **Let yourself cry:** A breakup is heart wrenching, and you deserve time to feel

lousy. It hurts. So give yourself over to
the agony and have a good cry. You'll feel
better. Scientific studies have shown that
tears actually excrete certain depression-
purging hormones so that you begin to
feel better physically and emotionally after
a good cry. It literally cleanses the soul.

Stop blaming yourself: People who
have been burned in a relationship too
often take the blame. They feel guilty
for failing at yet "another" relationship.
Eventually, they end up converting
their guilty feelings into an unhealthy
compulsion: overeating, abusing drugs or
alcohol, sexual trysts with near strangers,
or avoidance of intimacy altogether. Don't
get caught in the guilt trap. Although you
played a part in the relationship, you are
not the cause of its demise. It always
takes *two* people.

Beware of rebounding: Feeling rejected
by the person you care about is enough
to drive almost anyone into the arms of
the first willing person who comes along
after the breakup. This experience, in
fact, is so common that it has a name:

rebounding. But don't allow yourself to fall into this trap. If you do, you're only setting yourself up for another heartache. Research shows that those on the rebound tend to fall in love with people who will soon reject them. Don't let that be you.

12

Online Dating Is for You . . . If You Want to Safeguard Yourself from Emotional Pain and Danger

Your online dating safety begins with educating yourself.

—JOE TRACY

Do you know who makes the most money in the National Football League? The quarterbacks, running backs, and wide receivers. They also get the most headlines in the sports pages. But if you've read Michael Lewis's book *The Blind Side* or seen the movie by the same title, starring Sandra Bullock, you know that today the ones who earn the second-highest paychecks are left tackles.

Left tackles typically don't grab the headlines, but they play a vitally important position. Lewis traces their emerging importance back to the career-ending injury of star quarterback Joe Theismann on *Monday Night Football* in 1985. More than seventeen million people watched as an incredibly athletic linebacker named Lawrence Taylor blindsided Theismann, breaking his leg.

Since most quarterbacks are right-handed, the left tackle's main role is to prevent his quarterback from being hit from behind. And with the next generation of athletic linebackers and defensive ends, it takes a special person to do it. Left tackles must weigh more than three hundred pounds and have long arms to block, but they must also be quick on their feet. Today, teams are willing to pay for such a player. By 2004, the average salary of a left tackle in the NFL was $5.5 million a year. Only starting quarterbacks earned more.

Why? Because safeguarding the quarterback is essential to a team's success. Protection is a valuable asset—in any endeavor. And it's especially important when it comes to online dating.

You're More Protected Than You Think

One of the most frequent comments we hear from singles who are reluctant to get online to find love is that it's not safe. So let's admit it up front: Some of us have heard the stories, true or not, of people who have met weirdos on Web sites. These days, however, those stories are rare, and the reason is simple. The online dating industry has gotten smarter.

To show you how sophisticated and professional online dating services have become, they put a great deal of emphasis on privacy and anonymity. Of course, you have to give up a bit of your anonymity, but privacy is 100 percent guaranteed. And if you do happen to find someone undesirable who is bothering you, site moderators want to know about it. Your real name, address, phone number, and private e-mail address are never shared with anyone, unless *you* give it to someone online.

If your online friendship leads to an in-person date, follow the same rules you would in the traditional dating world if you were meeting someone for the first time: Choose a public meeting place, drive home alone, tell family and friends where you will be going and what time you expect to be home, and make sure your cell phone is running on a full battery. You may also want to have a friend call you at some point to check in—just in case you've been misled and the date is going poorly.

You Can End the Online Connection with a Click

Reputable dating sites that charge a fee for their services have the highest safety standards. In fact, most experts say that dating online is an extremely safe method of meeting other singles—much safer than meeting a stranger in public. In addition to letting you remain anonymous for as long as you like, these sites have blocker functions to prevent unwanted contact with certain singles. But here's the bottom line on safety in this area: You can find out much more about the other singles before a first date than you ever would if you had met randomly at a local church group or other venue. The online experience gives you a chance to learn about them before you actually meet—and that diminishes the potential for emotional disappointment as well as the potential for not being safe.

"It's really exciting to finally meet someone you have only been dating online," says Maggie, twenty-nine, "because over the Web, people are more apt to open up and let you see their true colors." It's true. In person, on a traditional first date, many people tend to be guarded and worried about how the other person is perceiving them. "When you are dating online, however," Maggie continues, "you simply have to click your mouse to get out of a conversation, and you know you will never have to see that person again, so you are more likely to be more vulnerable."

Being Smart about Being Online

Of course, in the same way that you let your guard down because you know the other people can't see you, they know you can't see them. That is why you occasionally hear stories about people meeting a date online who, in person, turns out to be nothing like his or her online persona. After all, it is quite easy to be an athletic and tall attorney online but in reality to be a pudgy, short student. Now, this is unlikely to be the case, but it's something to keep in mind.

Although the vast majority of people on reputable sites are genuine and honest, it's important to remember that, just as in traditional dating, you could encounter a misleading jerk. Simply be mindful of personal safety when it comes to the information you share online and in the initial stages of connecting in person.

Remember This

When we think about dating, often the first thing that comes to mind is the dinner-for-two experience featured in movies. But the dating experience—and especially the online dating experience—doesn't have to be a "solo" experience. The best dates are sometimes group dates. In group experiences, you can learn how your dating partner interacts with his or her friends—or yours. Those interactions can speak volumes about a person's true character. And if your friends meet your new date, they can also give you their first impressions. Consider making your first date a group experience. That can go a long way toward alleviating any safety concerns and also give you a variety of ways to get to know your date.

If you do decide to go on a one-on-one date, there are some things you can do to stay safe. Obviously, there is no need to suspect everyone of being dishonest online. But the following summary list of safety tips will help to ensure that your dating "blind side" is being protected:

> **Stay in control:** You should talk on the phone or meet in person only when you feel comfortable and ready. If the other person is being pushy, you have absolutely no obligation to comply.

> **Protect personal details:** Your last name, address, work details, and so on should remain private until you have established that the other person can be trusted. Much like in real life, it takes time to know people and to develop trust.

Ask for a recent photo: There's nothing wrong with asking people if their online photos are recent. If they haven't posted a photo, request one. And, of course, if you meet in person and your dates don't resemble their photos, you immediately know you're dealing with someone who is misleading and untrustworthy.

Meet the first time in a safe place: Your first meeting should be in an open, public, and familiar place, even if the other person sounds like a genuine, trustworthy person. This is not the time for a remote walk or drive.

Use a paid online dating service: Free online sites provide a greater opportunity for potentially dangerous individuals because those sites don't require a credit card or other information that can be used to identify the people using them.

Keep your friends in the know: A woman meeting an online date for the first time should tell a trusted friend or family member where she's going, with whom she is meeting, and perhaps ask her friend

to call her thirty minutes or so into the date
to check that everything is going okay.

Common sense rules: Obviously, avoid
anything that seems suspicious, weird, or
unsafe. You should probably heed your
instincts or gut feelings.[1]

Part 3

Five Questions You Absolutely Must Ask Before Signing Up

> He who asks a
> question is a fool
> for five minutes;
> he who does not
> ask a question
> remains a fool
> forever.
> —CHINESE PROVERB

13

Is the Site Dedicated to Helping Me Find True Love?

There is no more lovely, friendly and charming relationship, communion or company than a good marriage.

—MARTIN LUTHER

IN A *SEINFELD* EPISODE entitled "The Engagement," Jerry and his friend George Costanza have decided it's time to "grow up" and treat the women they date with a little more respect. (George has just broken up with a woman because she beat him in chess.) The conversation leaves such an indelible mark on George that he immediately looks up an old girlfriend, goes to her apartment, and asks her to marry him.

Jerry opts for something less extreme: He goes home to his apartment and decides to talk about the matter with his friend Kramer.

"I had a very interesting lunch with George Costanza today," Jerry says to Kramer. "We were talking about our lives, and we both kind of realized we're kids—we're not men."

Kramer says, "So then you asked yourselves, 'Isn't there something more to life?'"

"Yes!" Jerry says. "We did!"

"Well, let me clue you in on something," Kramer says. "There *isn't*."

"There isn't?" Jerry replies with a concerned look on his face.

"Absolutely not!" says Kramer. "I mean, what are you thinking about, Jerry? Marriage? Family? . . . They're prisons! Man-made prisons! You're doing time! You get up in the morning, she's there. You go to sleep at night, she's there. It's like you gotta ask permission to . . . to use the bathroom."

Kramer mocks the imaginary wife, saying with a sneer, "Is it all right if I use the bathroom now?"

"Really?" Jerry says.

"Yeah, and you can forget about watching TV while you're eating," Kramer says.

"I can?"

"You know why? Because it's 'dinner time'! You know what you do at dinner?"

"What?" Jerry asks.

"You talk about your day! 'How was your day

today? Did you have a good day today or a bad day today? What kind of day was it? I don't know. How about you? How was *your* day?"

"Boy," says Jerry.

To which Kramer replies, "It's sad, Jerry. It's a sad state of affairs."

Jerry is horrified at the picture that's been painted. "I'm glad we had this talk," he says to Kramer.

"Oh, you have no idea!" Kramer says.[1]

And neither does Kramer.

The Truth about Being Happily Married

Marriage is often fodder for sitcoms. And while we may laugh at Kramer's take on marriage, happily married couples know better. In fact, what Kramer called a "man-made prison" is actually the number one source of happiness on the planet. An emotional windfall awaits the people who find their right someone. Studies that follow people's lives over a number of years provide convincing evidence that marriage results in better emotional health. In practical terms, that means that married men and women have less depression, less anxiety, and fewer psychological problems in general. More important, people in good marriages have more fun.

One survey of fourteen thousand adults over a ten-year period found that 40 percent of married people say they are "very happy" with their lives in general, compared to fewer than 25 percent of those who are single or who are cohabiting. (Only 18 percent of divorced people fall into this category.)[2]

Finding Your Future Spouse Online

As we've said, for millions of singles, the online dating scene is often little more than a means to a hookup. In fact, as you probably already know, you can find site after site that is explicitly dedicated to flings and one-nighters. Now, we know that you're not looking for sites promoting the common meat-market mentality. We just want to be sure that as you're considering your options, you zero in on a site that is dedicated to helping you find love that lasts. That is, we want you to find a site that is focused on matching you for a relationship that can go the distance and lead you toward marriage.

Remember This

Not everyone is looking for "true love," and not every online dating site is dedicated to helping

people find it. Many singles have settled for
something significantly less—casual relationships
and one-night stands. They simply aren't looking
for someone to love for the rest of their lives.
When you go online to meet people, evaluate the
dating site you use to see if its values line up with
your own. It should act as your first filter. What
is the online site you are using doing to help you
find that right someone for you? The following
questions will help you determine whether the
people you meet online are serious about finding
their right someone:

Is my date becoming more open?

Don't expect deep conversations online
right away or on the first date. But over
time, ask yourself whether your date
is increasingly open about his or her
deepest-held beliefs and values and
willing to be emotionally vulnerable.

Does my date dream with me?

After
you have been dating for a while, it's
natural to start imagining the future. If
your date is starting to express hopes
and dreams for the future, that can be a
good sign that he or she is serious about
building a life together.

Is my date willing to spend time on me? Long-term commitments take time. People looking for the right one understand the importance of taking time to discover their dates fully. If your date is rushing you and you're starting to feel uncomfortable, that's a warning sign. Take a step back. It doesn't mean your date is the wrong one. It just means that you need more time to learn who your date really is and where he or she is headed.

14

Is the Site Truly Faith Based and in Sync with My Personal Beliefs?

Marriage calls for faith of the most radical sort.

—ELIZABETH CODY NEWENHUYSE

LAUREN LIKED ALEX—A LOT. They'd been dating for nearly four months, and her friend was asking about the relationship.

"So, is it getting pretty serious?"

Lauren, in her mid-thirties, just shrugged her shoulders and grinned.

"Oh, I know what that means—you *really* like him, don't you?"

"I do. We haven't said anything about being 'in love' yet, but the other night we were sitting on the couch watching TV, and he leaned over and kissed me," said Lauren. "I thought for sure he was going to tell me he loved me."

"Wow! You're in love, girl," her friend said.

"I know. He just seems so perfect."

"Why haven't you brought him to church with you?"

There was a moment of silence, and Lauren cringed. Then she said, "That's the one problem. He's not that into church."

"Oh, I see." Her girlfriend's eyebrows went up as the wheels in her mind started spinning.

Lauren quickly followed up with explanations of how she was going to eventually get him to church, but she didn't want him to feel uncomfortable. And the more she and her friend talked, the more apparent it became that Lauren's new boyfriend didn't have any interest in her Christian faith.

Should it matter? If you were in Lauren's shoes, would you feel uncomfortable about that?

Dating and the Christian Life

Let's take a moment and think this through on a simple level. Fact: If you are a follower of Christ, your relationship with God is the deepest, most profound, and most important part of your life. Fact: For a serious dating relationship to have any chance of success, you have to, in time, connect the most important parts of yourself with your potential spouse. Therefore, isn't it vitally important that the spiritual part of you be in sync with the spiritual part of your potential partner? Isn't that an essential element to "becoming one," soul to soul and heart to heart, in marriage?

Jesus prayed that his followers would be one in the same way that he and the Father are one (see John 17:11). And ultimately, that's the final purpose of dating—to find that person with whom we can walk with God. "If we don't feel some sort of conflict or loss because our date isn't on the same spiritual wavelength," says our friend Dr. John Townsend, coauthor of *Boundaries in Dating*, "there is a problem in our own religious life."[1] What he means is that if you don't see the setup for serious struggles in being "unequally yoked," as the old-fashioned phrase goes, you're having a tough time living out your Christian faith.

You see, the big question is not, How do our dating lives inform our spiritual lives? It's this: How do our spiritual lives inform our dating lives? Dating is a gift from God. He's the one who invented emotional connections, and he knows how they work best. That's why it's so important to follow his guidance by finding a date who shares the deepest and most important part of who we are. If we don't, we will inevitably end up feeling more like roommates than soul mates.

The Need to Start Out in Spiritual Sync

At the outset of this book, we told you that we were writing explicitly for Christian singles who take their faith seriously. So if that's you, we urge you to ensure that the dating site you use is committed to helping you find not only a lasting relationship but also a relationship that is grounded in the values of the Christian faith.

If you've studied God's Word, you already know that this is important from a theological perspective. But let us show you why it's important from a practical perspective as well. When a man and woman who both love God become husband and wife, they help each other on their Christian paths—"as iron sharpens iron."[2]

Consider the committed married couple who share a passionate Christian faith. They may struggle with doubts and spiritual dry spells, but on the whole, they are on a positive spiritual path together. Individually, they seek to know God and follow Jesus. But unlike so many other couples, these two have found ways to interact with each other on the spiritual plane, even in the midst of their fast-paced lives. Their individual spirituality is inspired by the sacred moments, be they ever so fleeting, that they share as a couple. Their religious behaviors are not mere rituals or duties; they are meaningful activities that bring them deep below the surface of the daily grind and then enable them to soar on the wings of shared spiritual experiences.

Our guess is that this is the experience you're longing for in your own eventual marriage. And you are likely to have already been committed to using a dating site that is operated by sincere Christians. We just felt compelled to make this point because we've counseled far too many couples who have been spiritual mismatches, and we've witnessed the heartache that can bring. That's why we want the very best for you—we want you to use a matching site that is populated with people who share your passion for living a life that honors God.

Remember This

Church attendance shouldn't be the only basis for being "equally yoked." What do your potential spouses really believe? How did they come to know Christ? How do they practice their faith? The answers to those questions can tell you even more about their relationship with Christ than the church they attend on Sundays.

Once you are using a matching site that values the Christian faith, you'll want to refine your filter for what will make the best match for you. In other words, just because a site is Christian doesn't mean that every person on the site is the kind of Christian you are looking for. So as you think about your right someone, carefully consider what issues related to faith are critical for you. The following are some of the most important to many people of faith. Use the following brief list to consider where you stand:

> **Prayer:** Is it important to you to find someone who has a consistent and meaningful prayer life? If so, what does that look like for you?

> **Denomination:** How important to you is it that your match come from a particular church denomination? If you've grown up a Baptist, for example, would it be a deal breaker if your potential match were a Methodist? Why or why not?

> **Tithing:** Is giving 10 percent of his or her income to the church a practice you see

as essential in your date? Why or why not?

Worship: How important to you is it that your date attend a weekly worship service? Would it matter to you, for example, if he or she attended monthly rather than weekly?

Devotions: Is it critical to you that your match have a routine and meaningful time of individual Bible study and meditation on God's Word? Would it bother you if he or she did not do this? Why or why not?

15

Does the Site Leverage My Personality for Maximum Matches?

There is little difference in people, but that little difference makes a big difference.

—W. CLEMENT STONE

READ ALMOST ANY online dating profile, and somewhere in it you will find something along the lines of, "I love to laugh" or "I've got a great sense of humor." It's almost inevitable.

And when you read what people are looking for in their perfect matches, they will often say something like, "I want someone who makes me laugh" or "I'm looking for someone who shares my quirky sense of humor."

Why is it that so many single people are looking for someone to laugh with? It has to do with personality. An individual's sense of humor is a little window into how his or her personality is hardwired. And most people have enough intuitive sense to know that in order to click with someone, they've got to share a sense of humor.

Research backs this inclination up too:

> Proverbs 17:22 says, "A cheerful heart is good medicine," and contemporary research seems to underscore this truth.
>
> Bob Hope made it to his 100th birthday, and so did George Burns. Coincidence? Maybe not, says Michael Irwin of UCLA's David Geffen School of Medicine. "Laughter releases endorphins—those 'feel good' hormones suspected of boosting immunity—and that might make you more resistant to disease."[1]

But laughter is more than good medicine when it comes to a person's love life. Sharing a similar sense of humor becomes a powerful glue between you. It helps you cope with tough times. It heals emotional wounds. Laughter is vitally important to lasting love. But here's the hitch: What's funny to some is not funny to others. Just because we say we have a good sense of humor, it doesn't mean we're going to be a good match for others who say the same thing in their dating profiles. We each laugh at different things because of our internal hardwiring.

In a survey of more than fourteen thousand participants who rated thirty jokes, the findings were unequivocal. "Every single joke," it was reported, "had a substantial number of fans who rated it 'very funny,' while another group dismissed it as 'not at all funny.'" Apparently our funny bones are located in different places. Some laugh uproariously at the slapstick of Larry, Moe, and Curly, while others enjoy the more cerebral humor of Woody Allen.[2]

That's where personality comes into the picture.

The Best Matches Are Based on Personalities

As public speakers, we've experienced occasions when someone laughs out loud at something almost everyone else barely gives a chuckle. And, of course, there are people who never crack a smile at something almost everyone else thinks is hilarious. What accounts for this? Personality differences. A sense of humor is just one of the many measurable factors within our personalities. Introversion and extroversion are other important factors, as are agreeableness, conscientiousness, curiosity, rigidity, perfectionism, devotion, impulsivity, the ability to delay gratification, and on and on.

Every autumn semester for many years running, I (Les) have taught a university class called Personality. You'll find this course in every undergraduate curriculum in every college in the country. It's a standard requirement for psychology majors. Scholars agree that this information is essential to a basic education in the science of psychology.

Leslie and I have come to believe that this information should also be required study for anyone who gets married, because the course is a study in individual differences. And when you study how people differ from one another, you can't help but understand how these differences can also be used to bring people closer together.

Personalities Are God Given

You can't choose your personality the same way you choose your wardrobe. Relatively speaking, you have just one personality for life. You are born with it. Sure, you can modify portions of your personality. And your response to your environment can cultivate or stifle aspects of it. But by and large, your personality represents your natural traits or tendencies. And every personality has strong points and weak points.

Your personality is in your genes. It is inborn. It is God given. You inherited a distinctive set of traits that are fundamental to your nature. You *can* behave in a way that does not represent your personality (even on dates, for example), but this will always be temporary. Any number of situations may require that you behave in a way that is not natural for you, but when the need has passed, you will once again act in a way that represents your true temperament. That's because your personality is innate.

Personalities Have Strong Points and Weak Points

For you to be at your best, you need to have your personality needs satisfied. For example, your personality may crave a detailed plan with time to think things through—whether it be for a major project at work or for an evening on the town. A well-thought-out plan makes you a happy camper. But if your "perfect match" stands in your way of having the time to craft a detailed plan for something you care about, you'll inevitably feel off kilter. And as your anxiety increases, you'll become irritable. Even worse, you'll become overly passive and clam up when you're asked for your input.

Or perhaps your personality craves quick results.

You're decisive. At work you make decisions quickly with confidence. You trust your instinct, and you shoot from the hip. You certainly don't waste time on small talk. But the moment your "perfect match" starts dragging you down by asking too many questions, you're bound to get more forceful. Maybe even boisterous and demanding.

Your Personalities Must Factor into Your Match

Are you getting the point? When it comes to personalities, our greatest strengths can become our greatest weaknesses—if our partner's personality traits do not complement our own. In other words, if your "perfect match" doesn't often meet the needs of your personality, you're going to have a very tough time of it. That why you've got to use a reputable matching site that has gone to the time and expense to take personality differences seriously. It can make all the difference for you.

Your eventual marriage will be the combination of two unique, powerful, and God-given personalities. Each personality brings a combination of strengths and weaknesses to the relationship. The mixture of these two sets of traits and temperaments creates a style of loving that will either work for you or work against you. If you marry the right someone—with the help of a dating site that leverages your personalities together—you will build a life together that is sure to weather tough times and bring you a lifetime of meaning and joy.

So relax and try to be your best self when chatting online and meeting face-to-face; you want to see if your personality fits with your potential mate's. And the only way to truly know is to be yourself.

Remember This

Although a quality site will use some kind of matching mechanism that delves into personality characteristics, you can also discover quite a bit from the photos people post of themselves on their profiles. The same is true of you. That's why we also want to note the value of selecting the best photos for optimal matching. With this in mind, you may find the following tips helpful:

> **Be sure the photo is accurate:** This may sound obvious, but one of the biggest complaints of online daters is that people's photos do not resemble them in real life. So why set up your date for

disappointment? Make sure your photo resembles the real you.

Make your photo recent: You may be tempted to post your favorite photo of yourself from eight years ago, but resist the urge. A good rule of thumb is to make sure your photo was taken within the past two years.

Be alone in your photo: Too many people make the mistake of posting photos that include other people. Naturally, this does prospective dates who are exploring your profile little good if they don't know which person is you. Why people do this remains a mystery. Please make sure your photo shows only you.

Don't post a "glamour" shot: If you've ducked into one of those mall-type studios where they dress you up and slather you with makeup for a photo session that makes you feel like a celebrity, refrain from posting this made-up version of yourself as your profile photo. Why? Because it's deceptive, and your prospects will see right through it.

Make sure your photo is happy: This, too, may sound obvious, but don't try to be a "drama llama" in your photo. You'll attract the best prospects with a photo in which you look as if you're having fun.

If you don't have any good photos, take some: So many people say they just don't have any photos to post. Well, it's never been easier to get a good head shot. You don't need to hire a professional. If you don't like the photos you have, get a friend to snap some shots of you—and keep snapping until you get something you like.

16
Does the Site Refine My Potential Matches for Me?

Less is more.

—LUDWIG MIES VAN DER ROHE

"WHEN I FIRST STARTED dating online, I thought the best part of it was having so many choices to consider," said Jenny. "It felt like an endless supply of guys to comb through, and if I wasn't careful, I could spend my entire evening just sitting at my computer looking at photos and reading profiles."

That's a typical response from someone new to online dating. Let's face it: After what may have been a long, dry spell of dateless Friday nights, a new cyberdater can feel like a kid being let loose in a candy store. You may be thinking, *What's wrong with that?* Well, once you dive into a huge ocean of countless online prospects, you soon discover exactly what's wrong with it. Before we spell it out, however, we want you to understand a little bit about the psychology of making choices. It can make a huge difference in how you might approach your online dating experience.

When Less Is More

In 2000, social psychologists at Columbia and Stanford were the first to demonstrate scientifically the disadvantages of having excessive choice. The research team showed that when shoppers are given the option of choosing among smaller and larger assortments of jam, they show more interest in the larger assortment, which really gets the shopper's attention. But when it comes time to pick just one jar of jam, shoppers are ten times more likely to make a purchase if they choose from among six rather than from among twenty-four flavors of jam.[1]

Did you catch that? If the consumers' choices were narrowed, they were far more likely to find what they were looking for. Maybe you're thinking that principle applies only to simple things, such as shopping for jam. Interestingly, when the stakes are higher, the same principle applies.

A recent study of how people go about making financial decisions regarding their future retirement proves the point. Researchers analyzed retirement-fund choices—ranging from packages of two to fifty-nine choices—among some 800,000 employees at 647 companies. "With 401(k)s, people are given enormous incentives to participate through tax shelters and employer matches," the researcher comments. "So, essentially, if you choose not to participate, you're throwing away free money."[2]

The article goes on to say, "Instead of leading to more thoughtful choosing, however, more options led people to act like the jam buyers: When given two choices, 75 percent participated, but when given 59 choices, only 60 percent did. In addition, the greater the number of options, the more cautious people were with their investment strategies. . . . Relatedly, too much choice also can lead people to make simple, snap judgments just to avoid the hassle of wading through confusing options."[3]

Here's the bottom line on all this: Numerous studies have found that the bigger the assortment, the harder it is for people to choose, except under one condition—when they enter the process with an articulated preference. And that's exactly why it's so important that you use an online dating site that refines your potential matches for you. The site refines your potential matches based on your "articulated preferences."

The More the Merrier?

Nearly everyone believes—wrongly—that more choices are always better. But as we've seen, studies have shown time and again that too many choices are just as bad as too few choices. Why? Because the more our brains have to search through, the more difficult it becomes to ignore irrelevant information. We are also more likely to be distracted by (or attracted to) attributes that were not initially relevant or pertinent to our original search—especially when it comes to online dating.

Marketing from online dating sites often suggests that having more choices is most beneficial because you have more options from which to choose. Of course, there's some truth in this. (We highlighted that fact in an earlier chapter.) But what they don't say is that the more options you have, the more work you have to do to find profiles that actually match what you're looking for.

For instance, imagine you're on an online dating site seeking men who have college degrees, are in a certain weight and body class, and want to have children. As you begin to search through the thousands of men who meet those criteria, you start noticing the color of a man's hair or his eyes, or that he went to Harvard instead of Ohio State. These distractions move you away from your original criteria and, in effect, ensure that you spend a lot more time searching than you would if the data set were smaller to begin with.

You may be thinking that's just fine, that you're happy to spend more time browsing through a million profiles. Well, okay, but it's not just more time you'll be spending. The research also shows that as your brain begins to search through so many potential choices, you are far more likely to make choices that are not optimal for you.[4] Our brains simply aren't very good at trying to sort through hundreds of possible choices, each with dozens or even hundreds of relevant attributes.

If you've spent a lot of time on dating Web sites, sifting through the myriads of choices, you don't need to be convinced of this fact. The best sites don't simply open the floodgates of possibilities to you without helping you refine your search for what matters most and then highlighting these potential matches for you. You are sure to find more success on a site that narrows your options based on what you've already determined to look for.

Remember This

As you are exploring potential matches online, you'll want to keep your considerations within the "realistic" realm. That is, you won't want to waste your time trying to look at every match possible. If you do, you'll drive yourself crazy. So here are some tips for staying on target:

Read the profile: Once you've discovered a profile and a picture that interest you, read, read, read! Many online dates don't do this. They make contact before they really know anything about the person they are contacting. Don't fall into this trap. You'll pick up a lot from a person's profile, so don't just "look at the pictures."

Stick to your deal breakers: As you are perusing the many options you have to choose from online, it can be tempting to explore some that are really not a good fit. Don't do it. You're only wasting your time. Keep your list of deal-breaking qualities in front of you so that you're looking only at serious contenders.

Ask others to weigh in: If you begin to feel as if you're at an ice cream store with

so many flavors that you can't decide, ask
what others think. They'll almost always
have an opinion. And by "others," we
mean people who love and care about
you. It's almost always helpful to have
their more objective input. And it's a sure
way to help you zero in on your best
options.

17

Does the Site Help Me Look beyond Just a Picture and a Paragraph?

Love is possible only if two persons communicate with each other from the center of their existence.

—ERICH FROMM

"I'VE BEEN LOOKING at dating profiles for a while now, and they are starting to sound the same," Rhonda said. "It's like digging through a table of sweaters at a garage sale and finding every sweater the same old same old—beige with a hole in the armpit."

Rhonda makes a good point. Online dating profiles can tell you only so much. Everyone seems to be witty, attractive, interesting, and intelligent. The men love moonlit walks on the beach and cooking a romantic, candlelit dinner for that special someone.

The women are relaxed, down to earth, fun, and into sports. Both the men and the women have so many wonderful hobbies and interests that it's a wonder they find any free time for dating. The kind of paragraph Rhonda is talking about would be accompanied by a dark photo of the person in the profile, with another person cropped out of it. A second photo is a distant shot of a person standing near a lake, and the paragraph would read something like this:

Okay, so I have to come up with at least one hundred words about myself. Well, I am an honest and creative person. I'm a Christian, and I love my church. I like to chill but am also spontaneous. I'm affectionate and fun loving with a good sense of humor. I can have fun doing almost anything. I'm not into drama or head games. I like meeting new people and exploring new places. I like to read sometimes, but I can't remember the last book I read. I'm a hard worker, and I love my job. I work a lot, but I play a lot too. When I'm not being a homebody, I love the outdoors and traveling. A great date can be staying at home with a movie

and popcorn, or a night on the town at a
nice restaurant. I'd really love to see Europe
someday. So that is a little about me. Did
I make a hundred words? So whaddya say?
Are you my match? Why don't we give it a
try and see?

We think you'll agree that you don't have to read too
many paragraphs like this one to become as bored as
Rhonda. The words reveal almost nothing about the
individual. In fact, the paragraph could describe any
number of people. That's why paragraphs like this,
filled with fluff, are almost useless.

Getting beyond the Bland Paragraph

Of course, some online daters do a far better job of
describing themselves and actually give a good idea
of who they are. They do that by providing some
specifics. Take a look at the following example:

I typically connect best with people who
are analytical. I am rarely offended by a
strong opinion, as long as the person can
back it up with facts. I'm committed to my
Christian faith and serious about walking
in the footsteps of Jesus. I run the AV stuff

at our church on a volunteer basis. I can come off as sarcastic sometimes, but it's all in good fun (so bring it on). I enjoy reading anything by Charles Colson, Philip Yancey, and Chuck Swindoll. I also like sci-fi movies, and I'm a bit of a history buff (especially on WWII). Compared to a lot of guys, I'm not that into sports unless I'm with people who are, though I do run regularly and ran a couple of marathons until my knee got messed up two years ago. If I sound like someone you'd be interested in, I'd love to meet you.

Whether you like the profile or not, you get a far better sense of who this person is than you do in the first example, right? Unfortunately, these kinds of straightforward descriptions are rare. Coye Cheshire and colleagues at the University of California–Berkeley have studied countless online dating profiles and observed that "while people think their tastes are distinct, most everyone's profile says they like fine dining, movies and long walks on the beach. . . . What's interesting about it is the way that we try to show that we're special and unique is that we like to do things just like everybody else."[1]

The Site Should Do This for You

Either way, whether a profile is as bland as a beige, secondhand sweater or as distinct as a brand-new argyle, a good dating site will take you past the pictures and paragraphs that a dater provides and create some clarity to help you gain a deeper understanding of a particular person and how well you might sync up. How? By combining your personality profile and a sophisticated way of aligning your preferences in an ideal match. You need not settle for anything less than a site that prioritizes matches based on what you're looking for and on what the science of relationship expertise prescribes.

Remember This

If you are giving serious consideration to trying out online dating, we want to leave you with some summary tips that will help you optimize your dot-com-dating experience. Of course, these are just a few of the most important items we've noted already in this booklet. So consider the following to be some true essentials for online success:

> **Be yourself:** This bears repeating. You'd never try to mislead someone you're dating in real life, so don't do it online. It

only short-circuits any potential you have for the real deal when meeting in person. Make sure your profile and your photo accurately represent you. After all, you want someone who falls in love with the real you, not with an illusion.

Be true to your values: This is so critical. If you are tempted to explore a relationship with someone who doesn't meet all your standards, you're only setting yourself up for eventual heartache. Don't put yourself through it. Keep your deal breakers in the forefront of your thinking as you're dating. Consider them to be your compass, and don't veer off course.

Tune in to your phony meter: If you are picking up a strange vibe from a prospective date, pay attention to it. This is a caution flag you shouldn't ignore. If you sense that a profile is not really authentic or you feel the person is too needy, or whatever, don't dismiss your intuitive thoughts. Do some more digging to see if there's something more that backs it up, and if so, move on.

Ask God for guidance: The most important thing you can do in the online dating process is to routinely and consistently ask God to help you make good decisions. Pray for guidance and wisdom with each potential match you consider.

Finale

Why We Cofounded MyRightSomeone.com

*Never be afraid to try something new. Remember, amateurs
built the ark. Professionals built the Titanic.*

—ANONYMOUS

AT THE START of this book we told you that after
years of studying the online dating experience,
after years of researching what works best, we felt
compelled to do more than write a book about it.
We decided to launch an online matching site that
would do everything we wanted it to. In the end, in
fact, the decision to launch such a site became more
of a calling, or even a compulsion.

We've dedicated much of our professional lives to
helping couples build strong and fulfilling marriages.
That began many years ago when we wrote a book

called *Saving Your Marriage Before It Starts*. Hundreds of thousands of couples have used this resource to prepare for married life together. The success of that book led to others, such as *Love Talk*, as well as efforts such as our Marriage Mentoring initiative that links seasoned couples with less-experienced couples in the local church. So it seemed only natural that our work would bring us to the place of launching an online matching site for Christian singles.

Our ministry is dedicated to seeing the divorce rate reduced dramatically in our lifetime and seeing stronger and more vibrant marriages, particularly among Christians. Nearly all our efforts are funneled toward this end. That's why the launch of this Web site, MyRightSomeone.com, is so important to us. You see, how well a couple matches—how two unique personalities come together and find love—can literally make or break that couple's chances for a meaningful and rewarding lifelong marriage together. So, as we said, we eventually felt compelled and called to launch MyRightSomeone.com.

The following characteristics are what make our site distinctive:

- MyRightSomeone is first and foremost thoroughly Christian. We are not inviting

anyone and everyone to use this site. It is
dedicated specifically for those singles who
hold a personal faith in God and have
committed themselves to walking with Jesus.

• The site is grounded not only on God's Word
but also on academic understanding. That
is, we aren't simply placing the proverbial
"God sticker" on our efforts and calling it the
Lord's work. We are drilling down on what
research reveals about God's truth in this
effort to match well and to build a successful
relationship that honors Christ.

• The site is dedicated to more serious relationships. We are not about helping people mix
and mingle just so they have dates on Friday
night (though that will obviously be a part
of this). We're invested in helping our users
find love. That means we aren't about simply
finding "someone" to fill a void. No. We are
about finding the "*right* someone" to fill a
lifetime.

• The site is not only dedicated to helping you
find the right someone, but it's also focused
on helping you *become* the "right someone."
Why? Because it's not enough to simply find
another single who meets your expectations
and preferences. This is the number one

mistake singles make, and it's the reason so many singles never find what they're looking for. They've neglected to focus on *who they are* as well as on what they want.

• Along these same lines, we are also dedicated to helping you hone the skills you need for a relationship that is all you want it to be. That is, we help you increase your odds of finding lifelong love by giving you the skills that research shows are critical to success.

All this may sound like a tall order, and it is. But that's why we have dedicated so much to making this service happen. If there were another site that did all of these things, we'd be pointing you to it. But since we couldn't find one, we've built it ourselves.

As you might imagine, launching this site was not a simple decision or an easy undertaking. It required an investment of time and money, along with a team of people who understood the mission and who had the expertise to help us build what we had in mind. Of course, it also required a lot of prayer.

And our prayer for you, whether you sign on to MyRightSomeone.com or not, is that you find the love God has planned for you and your life.

Notes

INTRODUCTION

1. Mark J. Penn, *Microtrends: The Small Forces behind Tomorrow's Big Changes* (New York: Twelve Publishers, 2007), 24.
2. Ellen McCarthy, "Marriage-Minded Do Better Online Than at Bars, Survey Claims," *Washington Post*, April 25, 2010, http://www.washingtonpost.com/wp-dyn/content/article/2010/04/23/AR2010042300014.html (accessed August 12, 2010).
3. Penn, *Microtrends*, 25.

CHAPTER 1

1. Joe Tracy, "Editorial: Online Dating—Is the Stigma Gone?" *Online Dating Magazine*, April 2006, http://www.onlinedatingmagazine.com/columns/2006editorials/04-onlinedatingstigma.html (accessed August 12, 2010).
2. Martin Lasden, "Of Bytes and Bulletin Boards," *New York Times*, August 4, 1985, http://www.nytimes.com/1985/08/04/magazine/of-bytes-and-bulletin-boards.html?sec=technology&spon=&pagewanted=2 (accessed August 12, 2010).
3. Heidi Stevens, "Chicago Couple Blazed the Trail for Internet Love," *Chicago Tribune*, May 18, 2008.
4. Meredith Farley, "Online Dating Becoming More Common in Seniors," *Your Retirement Living Connection,* June 16, 2010, http://www.retirementhomes.com/library/senior-living/retirement-living/online-dating-becoming-more

-common-in-seniors-201006161238.html (accessed August 13, 2010).

5. Leslie Gray Streeter, "Even Grandparents Find Success with Internet Matchmaking," *Palm Beach Post*, June 15, 2010, http://www.palmbeachpost.com/news/even-grandparents -find-success-with-internet-matchmaking-749473. html?printArticle=y (accessed August 12, 2010).

6. Mary-Anne Toy, "One in Four Adults Finds Mate Online," *Sydney Morning Herald*, April 17, 2010, http://www.smh .com.au/technology/technology-news/one-in-four-adults -finds-mate-online-20100416-skjk.html (accessed August 13, 2010).

7. Ellen McCarthy, "Marriage-Minded Do Better Online Than at Bars, Survey Claims," *Washington Post*, April 25, 2010, http://www.washingtonpost.com/wp-dyn/content/ article/2010/04/23/AR2010042300014.html (accessed August 13, 2010).

CHAPTER 2

1. "GPS Shows Couple True Love," WPBF.com, April 16, 2010, http://www.wpbf.com/news/23174248/detail.html (accessed August 13, 2010).

CHAPTER 3

1. Chris Lake, "Quechup Launches Worldwide Spam Campaign," E-consultancy.com, September 7, 2007, http://econsultancy.com/blog/1718-quechup-launches -worldwide-spam-campaign (accessed May 21, 2010).

2. Christian Rudder, "Why You Should Never Pay for Online Dating," *OkTrends*, April 7, 2010, http://blog.okcupid .com/index.php/why-you-should-never-pay-for-online- dating/.

CHAPTER 4

1. University of Kansas, "Online Daters Behave Similarly to Those Who Meet Face-to-Face, Researcher Says," *Science*

Daily, March 8, 2010, http://www.sciencedaily.com/releases/2010/03/100303131703.htm (accessed August 13, 2010).

2. J. T. Hancock, C. Toma, and N. Ellison, "The Truth about Lying in Online Dating Profiles," in *Proceedings of the ACM Conference on Human Factors in Computing Systems* (New York: Association for Computing Machinery, 2007), 449–52.

3. University of Kansas, "Online Daters Behave Similarly."

4. Jeffrey A. Hall and others, "Strategic Misrepresentation in Online Dating, The Effects of Gender, Self-monitoring, and Personality Traits," *Journal of Social and Personal Relationships* 27 (February 2010): 117–35.

5. University of Kansas, "Online Daters Behave Similarly."

CHAPTER 6

1. For a more detailed discussion, see Garry Friesen, *Decision Making and the Will of God: A Biblical Alternative to the Traditional View* (Portland, OR: Multnomah, 1980).

CHAPTER 7

1. Mary-Anne Toy, "One in Four Adults Finds Mate Online," *Sydney Morning Herald*, April 17, 2010, http://www.smh.com.au/technology/technology-news/one-in-four-adults-finds-mate-online-20100416-skjk.html (accessed August 15, 2010).

CHAPTER 8

1. Craig Wilson, "Many Singles Happy to Be Alone," *The Olympian*, October 25, 2001, http://news.theolympian.com/Census2000/128114.shtml (accessed August 15, 2010).

CHAPTER 9

1. Robert W. Firestone and Joyce Catlett, *Fear of Intimacy* (Washington, DC: American Psychological Association, 2000), 28.

CHAPTER 10

1. Bernice Kanner, "Are You Normal about Money?" *Ladies Home Journal*, October 1998.
2. Factoid in *U.S. News & World Report*, December 11, 1995.

CHAPTER 11

1. Peter Kramer, "Should You Leave?" *Psychology Today* (September 1, 1997), 38–45. See also http://www .psychology today.com/articles/199709/should-you -leave (accessed August 15, 2010).
2. Bruce Fisher, EdD, and Robert E. Alberti, PhD, *Rebuilding: When Your Relationship Ends* (Atascadero, CA: Impact Publishers, 1999).
3. Erich Fromm, *The Art of Loving* (New York: HarperCollins, 1989), 4.

CHAPTER 12

1. "Online Dating Safety," RSVP.com, www.rsvp.com.au/help/ safe +dating+tips.jsp (accessed August 16, 2010).

CHAPTER 13

1. *Seinfeld*, season 7, episode 111, "The Engagement," http:// www.youtube.com/watch?v=suAhGfVr_4U (accessed August 16, 2010).
2. James A. Davis, "New Money, an Old Man/Lady, and 'Two's Company': Subjective Welfare in the NORC General Social Surveys, 1972–1982," *Social Indicators Research* 15 (1984): 319–50.

CHAPTER 14

1. Henry Cloud and John Townsend, *Boundaries in Dating: Making Dating Work* (Grand Rapids: Zondervan, 2001), 50.
2. Proverbs 27:17.

CHAPTER 15

1. "Laughter *Is* the Best Medicine," Preaching Today. com, http://www.preachingtoday.com/illustrations/ weekly/07-05 -14/2051407.html (accessed August 16, 2010).

2. Dr. Les Parrott III and Dr. Leslie Parrott, *Questions Couples Ask: Answers to the Top 100 Marital Questions* (Grand Rapids: Zondervan, 1996), 69.

CHAPTER 16

1. Ira Smolowitz, PhD, "Consumer Marketing: A Flawed Strategy," http://www.apicsacramento.com/docs/ Consumer Marketing.pdf (accessed August 16, 2010).

2. Tori DeAngelis, "Too Many Choices?" *The APA Monitor* 35:6 (June 2004): 56.

3. DeAngelis, "Too Many Choices?"

4. P. L. Wu and Wen-Bin Chiou, "More Options Lead to More Searching and Worse Choices in Finding Partners for Romantic Relationships Online: An Experimental Study," *CyberPsychology & Behavior* 12:3 (June 2009): 1–4.

CHAPTER 17

1. Stephanie Rosenbloom, "The Ritual of the First Date, Circa 2010," *New York Times,* August 16, 2010, page ST1 of the national edition.

About the Authors

DRS. LES AND LESLIE PARROTT are founders and co-directors of the Center for Relationship Development at Seattle Pacific University (SPU), a groundbreaking program dedicated to teaching the basics of good relationships. Les Parrott is a professor of psychology at SPU, and Leslie is a marriage and family therapist at SPU. The Parrotts are authors of the Gold Medallion Award–winning *Saving Your Marriage Before It Starts, Becoming Soul Mates, Your Time-Starved Marriage, Love Talk, The Parent You Want to Be, Crazy Good Sex,* and *L.O.V.E.* The Parrotts have been featured on *Oprah, CBS This Morning,* CNN, and *The View,* and in *USA Today* and *The New York Times*. They are also frequent guest speakers and have written for a variety of magazines. Their Web site, **RealRelationships.com**, features more than one thousand free video-on-demand pieces answering relationship questions. Les and Leslie live in Seattle, Washington, with their two sons. They are cofounders of **MyRightSomeone.com**.